The Reader as DETECTIVE

LEVEL A
Second Edition

Burton Goodman
*Former Teacher of English and Coordinator of High
School–College Continuum, Bureau of Educational
and Vocational Guidance, New York City Public Schools*

AMSCO SCHOOL PUBLICATIONS, INC.
315 Hudson Street / New York, N.Y. 10013

Illustrations by John Jones

ISBN 1-56765-017-1

New York City Item 56765-017-0

Printed in the United States of America

11   04

TO THE STUDENT

The Reader as Detective has been specially designed to make you a more active reader—to help you become more involved in the reading process.

Today, more than ever, this is important because TV and movies can affect our reading habits. They, and other mass media, sometimes tend to make us passive, less active readers. This is unfortunate because reading is an active, participatory experience. It is not merely viewing or watching.

We believe that a good reader is an *active* reader, and that a good reader is like a good detective.

Think about this. When you read a powerful story of detection, suspense, mystery, or action, you march along with the characters in search of the ending, or solution. You *are*—or *should* become— THE READER AS DETECTIVE. Reading is an adventure—one in which you have become *involved*. Furthermore, the greater your involvement, the better reader you will become—and the more you will enjoy and appreciate reading.

This book will help make *you* THE READER AS DETECTIVE. It does this in a number of ways.

As noted above, the good reader must "march along with the characters in search of the ending, or solution." To encourage you to do this, each story in this volume contains a special and unique feature. It is called "Now it's time for YOU to be The Reader as Detective." This feature appears near the conclusion of each story. It provides you with an opportunity to be a reading detective—to guess how the story will end. After a while, you will learn to look for and discover clues and hints which will help you in this task.

A good reader is like a good detective in another way. To succeed, the detective must be able to gain an overall impression of the case, to recognize clues, identify important details, put events in sequence, draw inferences, and distinguish fact from opinion. Similarly, the effective reader must be a *reading* detective—on the search for the main idea, for supporting details, clues, inferences, and so forth. In a word, the reader, like the detective, must *master the skills* necessary to obtain successful results.

This volume provides ample opportunities for you to master these skills. Following each story are 25 short-answer questions. Questions 1 to 10 (**The Reader as Detective**) offer repeated practice in *the six basic reading skills* essential for achieving reading success. A symbol next to each question identifies the *kind* of reading skill that particular question helps you to develop. Each symbol is related to detection. Here are the symbols and the skills they represent:

THE SHERLOCK HOLMES HAT
    finding the *main idea*

A MAGNIFYING GLASS
    identifying *supporting details*

FINGERPRINTS
    finding *vocabulary clues*

A TRAIL OF FOOTPRINTS
    putting events in *sequence*

ILLUMINATED LIGHTBULB
    drawing *inferences*

SHERLOCK HOLMES PIPE
    distinguishing *fact from opinion*

Questions 11 to 15 (**On the Trail**) help you to track down and understand story elements such as plot, characterization, setting, style, tone, conflict, climax, irony, and theme.

Questions 16 to 25 (**Finding Word Meanings**) help you become a kind of word detective. By using context clues and Cloze (sentence completion and sentence context techniques), you will learn to develop vocabulary skills.

A final section (**Reviewing the Case**) offers a wide variety of interesting activities for discussion and writing—projects which will help you review the story.

The current edition contains a number of additional features including new and revised exercises, a Glossary, and easy identification of vocabulary words. To emphasize total communication skills (reading, writing, speaking, and listening), and to encourage cooperative activities, each **Reviewing the Case** section has been expanded.

The first story, "The Adventure of the Speckled Band," introduces the master detective, Sherlock Holmes. To help familiarize you with the format of this volume, the story has been divided into three parts. In each part, you will note the *techniques*, or skills, that Holmes uses to solve the case. You will be encouraged to use similar techniques as you read.

There are 18 stories in this volume, one for every week of the term—or every *other* week of the school year. The stories, and the exercises which follow them, are intended to help you develop an *active, participatory* approach to reading. We are convinced that they can help you develop a very special kind of reading habit—one which will serve you for a lifetime. Now, let's begin. It's time for *you* to become THE READER AS DETECTIVE.

Burton Goodman

ACKNOWLEDGMENTS

Grateful acknowledgment is made to the following sources for permission to reprint copyrighted stories. Adaptations are by Burton Goodman.

"After Twenty Years," page 35. From *The Four Million*, copyright 1904 by Press Publishing Co. Reprinted by permission of Doubleday & Company, Inc.

"The Open Window," page 43. From *The Complete Short Stories of Saki* (H. H. Munro). Copyright 1930, renewed © 1958 by The Viking Press, Inc. Adapted by permission of Viking Penguin, Inc.

"The Dinner Party," page 51. Bill Berger Associates, Inc., reprinted by permission of *Saturday Review* (January 31, 1942).

"A Secret for Two," page 75. By Quentin Reynolds. Copyright 1936, Crowell-Collier Publishing Company. Reprinted and adapted by permission of the Estate of Quentin Reynolds.

"Sarah Tops," page 84. © Copyright 1974 by Isaac Asimov. First published in *Boy's Life*, February 1975. Reprinted by permission of the author.

"One Throw," page 92. Reprinted by permission of William Morris Agency, Inc., on behalf of the author. Copyright © 1950 by Crowell-Collier Publishing Company, © 1978 by W. C. Heinz.

"The Leopard Man's Story," page 102. Copyright by Irving Shepard. Reprinted by permission of I. Milo Shepard, Trustee of Irving Shepard.

"The Fifty-First Dragon," page 110. From *The Collected Edition of Heywood Broun*, copyright by Heywood Hale Broun. Used by permission of Heywood Hale Broun and Patricia Broun and of Bill Cooper Associates Agency, Inc.

"August Heat," page 122. From *The Beast with Five Fingers—Twenty Tales of the Uncanny* by William Fryer Harvey. Copyright 1947 by E. P. Dutton and Company, Inc., and reprinted with their permission. Canadian rights by permission of J. M. Dent & Sons Ltd.

"Charles," page 131. From "Charles," included in *The Lottery*, copyright 1948, 1949 Shirley Jackson, renewed © 1976 by Laurence Hyman, Barry Hyman, Mrs. Sarah Webster, and Mrs. Joanne Schnurer. Reprinted by permission of Farrar, Straus and Giroux, Inc. Adaptation by the editors of *Scope English Anthology, Level Two*, copyright © 1979, 1983 by Scholastic Inc., reprinted by permission.

"Raymond's Run," page 139. Copyright 1970 © by Toni Cade Bambara. Adapted by Burton Goodman with the permission of Random House, Inc., from *Gorilla, My Love*, by Toni Cade Bambara. Reprinted by permission of the author.

"The Chaser," page 150. Copyright 1940, © renewed 1967 by John Collier. Reprinted by permission of the Harold Matson Company, Inc.

"The Lather and Nothing Else," page 158. English translation from *Américas*, January 1956. Reprinted by permission of Organization of American States.

CONTENTS

The Reader as DETECTIVE

"Her face was pale, with restless, frightened eyes,
like those of some hunted animal."

The Adventure of
the Speckled
Band

PART 1

by Arthur Conan Doyle

For the past eight years, I have studied more than 70 cases solved by my good friend, Sherlock Holmes. Some of them were funny. Others were quite strange. But not one was ordinary. Of his many cases, however, I can think of none more unusual than "The Adventure of the Speckled Band."

It began early in April in the year of 1883. I was sharing rooms with Holmes on Baker Street in those days. A sudden noise awoke me one morning. I looked up to find Sherlock Holmes standing, fully dressed, by the side of the bed. The clock showed that it was just a quarter past seven.

"Very sorry to wake you up, Watson," said Holmes. "I was awakened early myself."

"What is it, then? A fire?"

"No, it seems a young lady has arrived. She is very upset. She insisted upon seeing me and is now waiting in the sitting room."

3

I looked at Holmes with growing interest.

"I can tell you this, Watson," he continued, "when young ladies wander about the city at this hour of the morning, when they get sleepy people out of their beds, they must have something important to say. This may prove to be an interesting case, Watson. You may wish to follow it from the start. I thought I should wake you and give you that chance."

"My dear fellow, I would not miss it for anything."

I quickly put on my clothes. In minutes I was ready to accompany my friend to the sitting room. A lady dressed in black rose as we entered.

"Good morning, madam," said Holmes cheerfully. "My name is Sherlock Holmes. This is my good friend and companion, Dr. Watson. You may speak as freely before him as before me."

Holmes glanced across the room to the fireplace. "I am glad to see such a roaring fire," he said. "Please pull your chair up to it, for I observe that you are shivering."

"It is not the cold which makes me shiver," the woman said in a low voice.

"What is it then?"

"It is fear, Mr. Holmes. It is terror."

She raised her veil as she spoke, and we could see that her words were true. Her face was pale, with restless, frightened eyes, like those of some hunted animal.

Holmes bent forward. "You must not fear," he said soothingly. "We shall, I am sure, soon set matters right. You have, I see, come in by train this morning."

She looked at him with surprise. "Do you know me, then?"

"No, but I observe the second half of a return ticket in the palm of your left glove. You must have started early. Yet you had a long drive in a cart, along muddy roads, before you reached the station."

The lady stared in surprise at my companion.

"It is no mystery," said Holmes, smiling. "The left arm of your jacket is splattered with mud. The marks are quite fresh. No vehicle but a cart throws up mud that way—and then only when you sit on the left-hand side of the driver."

"Whatever your reasoning may be, you are perfectly correct."

The lady suddenly sat up straight in her chair. "Mr.

Holmes," she said, "I have heard of you. Perhaps you can help me. Perhaps you can throw a little light on the darkness that surrounds me."

She paused. "At the moment I cannot pay you for your services. But in a month or six weeks I shall be married and shall have my own money. I can pay you then."

"I can only say, madam," replied Holmes, "that I shall be happy to take your case. You may pay me when it pleases you. Now tell us everything that may help us."

"My name is Helen Stover," she said. "I live with my stepfather. He is the last of the Roylotts of Stoke Moran, a famous family in England."

Holmes nodded his head. "The Roylotts," he said. "I have heard the name."

"Once," she said, "the family was rich and their lands stretched far. Little, however, is left today. A small piece of land and a very old house are all that remain.

"My stepfather became a doctor," said Miss Stover. "He went to India. It was in India that Dr. Roylott married my mother. My father had died when my twin sister Julia and I were only two years old. Soon after, my mother was killed in a railroad accident. She was very wealthy and left all her money to Dr. Roylott. But the will stated that a certain sum of money would be given to each of us when we married."

"And how large a sum was that?" asked Holmes.

"That I do not know," replied Miss Stover. "But I believe it may be considerable."

"I see," said Holmes.

"Dr. Roylott then left India. My sister and I went to live with him in the old house at Stoke Moran."

Helen Stover shook her head sadly. "At Stoke Moran our stepfather changed completely. He shut himself up in the old house. He seldom went out. When he did venture forth, he fought with whoever happened to cross his path. As you can imagine, he was not very popular. People ran from him when he came near, for he is a man of very great strength.

"He has no friends at all, Mr. Holmes—except for a few wandering vagabonds. He lets them stay on his land. But he does love animals from India. They are sent to him from that country. He has a cheetah and a baboon, which roam freely over the grounds. The villagers are almost as afraid of the animals as they are of my stepfather.

"You can guess that my poor sister Julia and I did not have much pleasure in our lives. She was only thirty at the time of her death. Yet her hair was already turning white."

"Your sister is dead, then?" said Holmes.

"She died two years ago. It is because of her death that I came to speak to you.

"Two years ago, at Christmas, we were visiting a relative near London. There Julia met a man who wanted to marry her. My stepfather agreed. But two weeks before the wedding something terrible happened."

Sherlock Holmes looked closely at his visitor. "Please," he said, "explain exactly what occurred."

"I can do that easily," said Miss Stover, "for I shall never forget that fatal day. As I have told you, the house is very old. Only three bedrooms are now in use. They are all on the ground floor. The first is my own, the second my sister's, and the third Dr. Roylott's. The bedrooms are all side by side, though there are no doors between them. But they all open out to the same hall. Am I making myself clear?"

"Perfectly."

"The windows of the three rooms look out upon the garden. That fatal night, Dr. Roylott had gone to bed early. He was not yet asleep, however. My sister was bothered by the smell of the Indian cigars which he likes to smoke. She, therefore, left her room and came into mine. We sat there chatting.

"'Tell me, Helen,' she said, 'have you ever heard anyone whistling in the middle of the night?'

"'Never,' said I.

"'Is it possible that you whistle in your sleep?'

"'Certainly not. But why?'

"'For the last few nights,' said she, 'I have been awakened by a low, clear whistle. I cannot tell where it came from— perhaps from the room, perhaps from the garden. I thought that I would ask you if you had heard it.'

"'No,' I answered, 'it is probably the vagabonds on the grounds.'

"'Very likely. Yet I'm surprised that you didn't hear it, too.'

"'Ah, but I sleep more heavily than you.'

"'Well, it doesn't matter.' She smiled at me and closed the door. A few moments later, I heard the key turn in her lock."

"Indeed," said Holmes. "Did you always lock your doors at night?"

"Always."

"And why?"

"I think that I mentioned to you that Dr. Roylott had a cheetah and a baboon. We did not feel safe unless our doors were locked."

"Quite so. Please go on." said Holmes.

"I could not sleep that night. A storm raged. Outside, the wind was howling, and the rain beat against the windows. Suddenly, in the middle of the gale, I heard the wild screams of a terrified woman. I knew at once that it was my sister's voice.

"I jumped from the bed and rushed into the hall. As I opened my door, I seemed to hear a low whistle. Then I heard a clanging sound, as if something made of metal had fallen. As I ran down the hall, I saw my sister's door open. By the light of the lamp, I saw my sister at the opening. Her face was white with terror.

"I ran to her and threw my arms around her. But her knees seemed to give way and she fell to the ground. Then she screamed, in a voice which I shall never forget. 'Helen! It was the band! The speckled band!' She pointed in the direction of the doctor's room, but could say no more.

"I rushed out, calling loudly for my stepfather. I met him hurrying from his room. But, by the time he reached my sister's side, she had already died. Such was the dreadful end of my beloved sister."

"One moment," said Holmes. "Are you sure about the whistle and the sound of metal that followed?"

"I believe so," said Miss Stover. "And yet, I cannot say so with confidence. With the noise of the storm, I may have been mistaken."

"Did the police investigate?" asked Holmes.

"Very carefully. But they could not find the cause of my sister's death. Her door had been locked from the inside, and the shutter of her window was locked with a strong iron lock. The walls and the floor were also found to be solid. It is certain, therefore, that Julia was alone when she met her end.

Furthermore," continued Miss Stover, "there were no marks of any kind on her."

"What about the possibility of poison?" asked Holmes.

"The doctor found no sign of it."

Holmes thought for a moment. "What do you think your sister died of?" he asked.

"It is my belief that she died of shock," said Miss Stover. "Though what it was that frightened her I cannot imagine."

"And what," asked Holmes, "did she mean by 'the band. The speckled band'?"

"I do not know. It may refer to a band of people—vagabonds who camp on our land. Many of them wear spotted-speckled-handkerchiefs over their heads."

Holmes shook his head and looked doubtful. "Please go on with your story," he said.

"Two years have passed since then. My life has been lonelier than ever until lately. A month ago, a dear friend whom I have known for years asked me to marry him. My stepfather has agreed and we are to be married in the spring. Two days ago some repairs were started in the house. I had to move into the bedroom in which my sister died, to sleep in her bed.

"Imagine then my terror when I suddenly awoke, and heard, in the silence of the night, the low whistle my sister had described. I jumped up and turned on the lamp. There was nothing in the room. I was too upset to go back to bed, however. I dressed, and left the house as soon as it was daylight. I decided to come here to ask your help."

"You have acted wisely," said Holmes. "We must move quickly. There is not a moment to lose. We must leave at once for Stoke Moran!"

Now it's time for *you* to be a reading detective. The following exercises will help you accomplish this. Like Sherlock Holmes, you will learn to look for clues, find details, put events in sequence, and so forth. You will also learn to *anticipate*, or think ahead.

I. The Reader as Detective

Read each of the following questions. Then write the letter of the correct answer to each question. Remember, the symbol next to each question identifies the *kind* of reading skill that particular question helps you to develop.

Let's review the symbols.

 ...finding the *main idea*

 ...identifying *supporting details*

 ...finding *vocabulary clues*

 ...putting events in *sequence*

 ...drawing *inferences*

 ...distinguishing *fact from opinion*

 1. Holmes woke Watson because
     a. Holmes wanted to leave for his office.
     b. it was already a quarter past seven.
     c. a new client had arrived.

 2. Helen Stover was shivering because she was
     a. ill.   *b.* frightened.   *c.* cold.

 3. Holmes observed fresh marks on his visitor's jacket. As used in this sentence, what is the meaning of the word *fresh*?
     a. outspoken   *b.* untried   *c.* new

4. Which happened last?

   a. Julia Stover died.
   b. Dr. Roylott went to India.
   c. Helen Stover moved into her sister's bedroom.

5. We may infer that Watson followed Holmes's cases

   a. with great interest.   *c.* now and then.
   b. with little interest.

6. "We did not feel safe unless our doors were locked." Which word or expression best defines the word *safe* as used in this sentence?

   a. warm   *c.* a place to keep valuables
   b. free from danger

7. Which expression best describes the night on which Julia Stover died?

   a. calm and peaceful   *c.* bright and sunny
   b. wild and stormy

8. At the end of the story, Helen Stover probably felt

   a. sorrowful   *b.* ill   *c.* relieved

9. Which of the following statements expresses an opinion?

   a. The case began in April.
   b. The Roylott family was once very wealthy.
   c. It was certain that Holmes would solve the case.

10. Which of the following is the best title for the chapter?

   a. A Strange Case Begins
   b. I Hate Working Early
   c. Truth Is Stranger Than Fiction

II. On the Trail

STORY CLUES

How well do you spot *story clues?* Story clues are hints or signposts that point the way to how the story will end. As you read, learn to look for and to recognize story signs.

Each of the following questions is based on a story clue found in the selection. The correct answers play an important part in the story. They can help you solve the mystery of "The Speckled Band."

11. Mrs. Stover's will stated that each daughter would
   a. receive a certain sum of money on marrying.
   b. receive a small piece of land.
   c. share the family's riches with their stepfather.

12. Which one of the following statements is true of Dr. Roylott?
   a. He often visited relatives.
   b. He received animals from India.
   c. He was admired by his neighbors.

13. Julia Stover died
   a. in a railroad accident.
   b. two weeks before her marriage.
   c. a month after her wedding.

14. On the night of her sister's death, Helen Stover heard
   a. a low whistle and a clanging sound.
   b. something banging against the door.
   c. vagabonds shouting in the garden.

15. Because of repairs in the house, Helen had to sleep
   a. at an inn.
   b. in a tent on the grounds.
   c. in her sister's bed.

Review your answers to the questions above. Keep these story clues in mind when you read Part 2 of the story. As you continue to read, look for other story clues. You are on your way to becoming a better reader—or mystery solver.

III. Finding Word Meanings

Following are ten words which appear in Part 1 of "The Adventure of the Speckled Band." Study the words and the definitions beside them. Then complete the following paragraphs by using each vocabulary word only *once*.

The first two words have already been added. They will help you get started. Now you're on your own!

page

ordinary	common; not special	3
companion	one who shares in what another is doing	4
observe	see and note; study	4
soothingly	calmly; quietly	4
vehicle	any means of carrying, communicating, or making known	4
popular	liked by most people	5
pleasure	enjoyment; delight	6
fatal	causing death or ruin	6
confidence	strong belief in oneself	7
described	told in words	8

Sherlock Holmes is hardly an [16] _ordinary_ detective. He is probably the most [17] _popular_ detective ever created. Through the years, his adventures have given __18__ to millions of readers.

It is great fun to study or __19__ Sherlock Holmes at work. No matter how difficult the case appears to be, he approaches it with __20__ . He carefully searches for clues which will prove __21__ to those who are guilty. Then the master detective very calmly and __22__ explains how he solved the mystery.

Doctor Watson serves as the __23__ for communicating the tales of Sherlock Holmes. Each adventure is __24__ by Dr. Watson. He is Holmes's friend and __25__ .

IV. Reviewing the Case

Now, it's time to review the case. Answer each of the following questions by using complete sentences. Each of your answers should contain at least _two_ facts found in the story.

A. How did Holmes know that Helen Stover had arrived by train after riding in a cart along muddy roads?

B. Why did it seem impossible for anyone to have murdered Julia Stover?

C. Read the last paragraph of the story again. Give your reasons for Holmes's statement.

The Adventure of the Speckled Band

PART 2

"Yes," continued Holmes, "we have not a moment to lose. If we were to come to Stoke Moran today, could we see the rooms without your stepfather's knowing it?"

"As it happens," said Miss Stover, "he spoke of coming to London today on business. He will probably be away all day, so you could look around undisturbed. We have a housekeeper now, but I can easily get her out of the way."

"Excellent. Do you mind making the trip, Watson?"

"No, not at all."

"Then we shall both come."

Holmes turned to his visitor. "When do you plan on returning?" he asked.

"I have one or two things which I would like to do in town. But I shall return by the twelve o'clock train to be there when you arrive."

"You may expect us in the afternoon. I, too, have some matters to attend to. But will you have some breakfast first?"

"No, I must go. But my heart is much lighter now that I have spoken to you. I look forward to seeing you again this afternoon."

With that, Miss Stover dropped the black veil over her face, and left the room.

Sherlock Holmes leaned back in his chair. "And what do you think of it all, Watson?" he inquired.

"It seems to me a dark and evil business."

"Dark enough and evil enough."

"But if the door and windows were locked, and the floor and walls were solid, then the lady must surely have been alone when she met her mysterious end."

"What, then, of those whistles in the night?" said Holmes. "And what of the strange words of the dying woman?"

"I cannot imagine."

"To find the answers, we are going to Stoke Moran today. I want to see—but what in the name of the devil!"

Our door had suddenly been thrown open and a huge figure of a man stood framed in the doorway. He was wearing a black top hat and a long, dark coat. So tall was he that his hat actually brushed against the top of the doorway. His large face was covered with a heavy dark beard and his eyes blazed at us with hatred.

"Which one of you is Holmes?" asked the figure.

"That is my name, sir. But you have the advantage over me," said my companion softly.

"I am Dr. Grimesby Roylott of Stoke Moran."

"Indeed, doctor," said Holmes. "Please take a seat."

"I will do nothing of the kind. My stepdaughter has been here. I have traced her. What has she been saying to you?"

"That I cannot tell you," said Holmes

"What has she been telling you!" shouted the man furiously.

"It is a little cold for this time of year," said Holmes.

"Ha! You put me off, do you?" said our visitor, taking a step forward and shaking his fist. "I know you, you mischief-maker! I have heard of you before. You are Holmes, the meddler!"

My friend smiled.

"Holmes, the busybody!"

His smile grew wider.

"Holmes, the nuisance!"

Holmes chuckled loudly. "Your conversation is most

amusing," said he. "On your way out, please close the door for I feel a draft."

"I will go when I have said my say. Don't you dare to become involved in my affairs, Mr. Holmes! I know that Miss Stover had been here. I traced her! I am a dangerous man to fool with. See here!"

Dr. Roylott stepped swiftly to the fireplace. He seized the poker and bent it into a curve with his powerful hands.

"See that you stay out of my way!" he snarled. Then, hurling the twisted poker into the fireplace, Dr. Roylott marched out of the room.

"He does not seem a very friendly person," said Holmes. "I am not quite so large as he, but if he had remained, I might have shown him that my grip is not much weaker than his own." As Holmes spoke, he picked up the steel poker, and with a sudden twist, straightened it out again.

"And now, Watson," said Holmes, "we shall order breakfast. And afterwards I hope to obtain some information which may help us greatly. Then we must be on our way to Stoke Moran."

It was a perfect day. The sun was bright and a few fluffy white clouds hung in the sky. The trees and flowers were showing their first green shoots. The air was filled with the rich smell of the earth. Holmes had hired a cab, and we were on our way to Stoke Moran.

For much of the journey, my friend had been sitting quietly. His arms were folded and his hat was pulled down over his eyes. He seemed to be buried in the deepest of thought. Suddenly Holmes spoke.

"I have seen Mrs. Stover's will," he said.

"Her daughter spoke of it."

"Yes," said Holmes. "The will states that each of Mrs. Stover's daughters is to receive a large sum of money on the day that she marries."

"Who is in possession of the money now?"

"Dr. Roylott. This proves, without a doubt, that he had very strong reasons for preventing them from marrying."

The driver suddenly interrupted. "Look there," said he, pointing over the meadows. On the top of a heavily wooded piece of land stood a very old mansion.

"Stoke Moran?" said Holmes.

"Yes, sir. That is the house of Dr. Grimesby Roylott."

"That is where we are going," remarked Holmes.

"There's the village just to the left," said the driver. "But if you want to get to the house, the quickest way is to hop over that wall and take the footpaths through the fields."

"We will do as you suggest," said Holmes.

We got out, paid our fare, and the cab rattled back on its way.

Minutes later, we were greeted at the door by Miss Stover, who had seen us through a window.

"I have been waiting for you eagerly," she said, shaking hands with us warmly. "All has turned out splendidly. Dr. Roylott has gone to London. He will probably not be back before evening."

"We have had the pleasure of meeting the doctor," said Holmes. And in a few words, he explained what had happened.

"He has followed me then," said Miss Stover.

"So it appears," replied Holmes. "We must see to it that you are safe from him tonight. But for now, we must make the best use of our time. Kindly take us to the rooms we are to examine."

Miss Stover led us through the building to the three rooms she had spoken of earlier. They stood side by side. We stepped into the first.

"This, I take it," said Holmes, "is your room. The center one must be your sister's, and the last one, Dr. Roylott's."

"Exactly. But I am sleeping in the middle one now."

"Because of the repairs, as I understand."

"Yes," said Miss Stover. "But I believe that was just an excuse to get me out of my room and into my sister's room."

Holmes looked around the room. "Ah, that is interesting," he said as he moved to the window. The shutters in front of it were solid, and held in place by a strong iron lock. "Hmm," said Holmes, "no one could have gotten in this way if the shutters were locked. Yet, since you both locked your doors, no one could enter from that direction either."

We moved down the hall into the second room—the one in which Miss Stover now slept. It was the room in which her sister had met her sad fate. It was a gloomy little room with a low ceiling and a large fireplace. A brown chest of drawers stood in one corner, a narrow bed in the other. There was a dressing table along with two small chairs. These made up all the furniture in the room.

Holmes pulled one of the chairs into a corner and sat silently. His eyes traveled round and round, up and down, taking in every detail of the apartment. At last, he pointed to a thick bell rope which hung down near the bed. The end of it was actually lying on the pillow.

"That bell rope," he asked, "where does it go?"

"It goes to the housekeeper's room," said Miss Stover. "It can be used to ring for her."

"I see. It looks newer than the other things in the room."

"Yes, it was put there only two years ago."

"Your sister asked for it, I suppose," said Holmes.

"No, my sister was very active. I never heard her use it to ring for anything. We always got what we wanted for ourselves."

"Indeed. Then it hardly seems necessary to have put a bell there."

From his pocket, Holmes drew a magnifying glass. "You

will excuse me for a few minutes," he said, "while I satisfy myself about this floor." He threw himself down upon his face and crawled swiftly backward and forward, carefully examining the cracks between the boards. Then he did the same with the woodwork on the walls.

"The floor and walls are sound," said Holmes, walking over to the bed. He spent some time staring at it. Then he ran his eyes up and down the wall. Finally, he took the bell rope in his hand and briskly gave it a pull.

There was no sound.

"Why, it's a dummy," said Holmes.

"Won't it ring?"

"No, the bell is not even attached at the top. This is very interesting," said Holmes. "If you look very carefully, you can see that the rope is tied to a hook just above where the little opening of the air ventilator is."

"I never noticed that before," said Miss Stover.

"Strange," said Holmes. "What a fool the builder was to put an air ventilator between two rooms. With a little more trouble, he might have built it so that it would reach the fresh air outside."

"The ventilator is also quite modern." said Miss Stover.

"Done about the same time as the bell rope?" remarked Holmes.

"Yes, there were several little changes made about that time."

"That is something to reflect about," said Holmes. "And now, Miss Stover, with your permission, let us look at Dr. Roylott's room."

Dr. Grimesby Roylott's room was larger than the other two. However, it was furnished as simply. It contained a bed, a shelf full of books, and a large iron safe. A plain wooden chair rested against a wall.

Holmes examined each object carefully. "What's in here?" he asked, tapping the safe.

"My stepfather's business papers."

"There isn't a cat in it, for example."

"Why, no. What a funny idea."

"Well, look at this," said Holmes. He pointed to a small saucer of milk which stood on top of the safe.

"No, we don't have a cat. But there are a cheetah and a baboon."

"Ah, yes, of course. Well, you might consider a cheetah just a big cat. Still, I should think, a saucer of milk won't go very far in satisfying its hunger."

Holmes bent down in front of the wooden chair. "There is one point," he muttered to himself, "about which I should like to be quite positive." He carefully examined the seat of the chair. "Thank you," he said, after a while. "That is quite settled." He returned the magnifying glass to his pocket.

"Hello," said Holmes. "Here is something interesting." The object which had caught his attention was a small dog leash which lay on one corner of the bed. The leash, however, was curled up and tied at the end so that it made a small, tight loop.

"What do you make of that, Watson?"

"It's a common enough dog leash. But I don't know why it should be looped at the end."

"That is not quite so common, is it?" said Holmes. "Ah me, it's a wicked world. And when a clever man turns his head to crime, it's the worst of all. I think that I have seen enough, Miss Stover."

My friend's face had turned grim. "It is very important, Miss Stover," said he, "that you follow my advice carefully. Your very life may depend on it."

Miss Stover and I gazed at Holmes in astonishment. He walked to the window, unlocked the shutters, and looked out. "I believe," said Holmes, "that is the village inn over there."

"Yes," said Miss Stover. "It is known as the 'Crown.'"

"Very good," said Holmes. "And would it be possible to see the window of your room from there?"

"Of course."

"Excellent," said Holmes, "that is where Dr. Watson and I will wait. Now, Miss Stover, you must lock yourself in your room when your stepfather comes home. Do not see him at all. Then, when you hear him go to bed for the night, you must open the shutters of your window. Place a lighted lamp in the window. That will be the signal to us in the Crown. Quickly, then, go back to the room you used to sleep in. I believe that, in spite of the repairs, you could manage there for one night."

"Oh, yes," said Miss Stover. "Easily."

"Leave the rest in our hands."

"But what will you do?"

"We shall spend the night in your room. There we shall continue our investigation of the noise that has disturbed you."

"I believe that you have already made up your mind about what it was," said Miss Stover.

"Yes," said Holmes. "But I would prefer to have some proof before I speak."

"Tell me, at least," said Miss Stover, "if you believe my sister died of fright."

"No, I do not think so," said Holmes. "I believe there was another cause. But for now, Miss Stover, we must leave you. If our plan works, we shall soon have all the proof we need."

Now it's time for YOU to be The Reader as Detective

Do you have any idea of how Julia Stover died? What, or who, might have killed her? Try the following exercises. Then read the conclusion to "The Adventure of the Speckled Band."

I. The Reader as Detective

Read each of the following questions. Then write the letter of the correct answer to each question. Remember, the symbol next to each question identifies the *kind* of reading skill that particular question helps you to develop.

1. Dr. Roylott was wearing

    a. a brown top hat.   *c.* a long, dark coat.

    b. a black sweater.

2. "All has turned out splendidly," said Helen Stover happily. What is the meaning of the word *splendidly*?

    a. very well   *c.* very suddenly

    b. very poorly

3. Holmes looked carefully at the woodwork on the walls because he

  a. liked the pattern very much.
  b. thought he had dropped something there.
  c. wanted to see if anyone might have come in that way.

4. Which happened first?

  a. Holmes and Watson took a cab to Stoke Moran.
  b. Holmes examined the chair with a magnifying glass.
  c. Holmes decided to rent a room at the village inn.

5. Holmes told Helen Stover to

  a. say hello to her stepfather as soon as he returned.
  b. lock herself in her room when her stepfather came home.
  c. spend the night at the "Crown."

6. Which of the following statements expresses a fact?

  a. The shutters were held in place by a strong lock.
  b. Dr. Roylott was probably hiding somewhere in the house.
  c. Holmes believed that Julia Stover died of fright.

7. In all, how many rooms did Holmes examine?

  a. two rooms
  b. three rooms
  c. four rooms

8. We may infer that

  a. Miss Stover was in great danger.
  b. Holmes was in no hurry to visit Stoke Moran.
  c. Watson had already solved the mystery.

9. Holmes told Dr. Roylott, "On your way out, please close the door for I feel a draft." Which expression best defines the word *draft* as used in this sentence?

  a. rough copy
  b. plan or sketch
  c. current of air

10. Which sentence best expresses the main idea of the selection?

   a. All of the rooms were furnished very simply.
   b. Holmes looked for clues and thought of a plan.
   c. Dr. Roylott bent a poker and hurled it into the fireplace.

II. On the Trail

STORY CLUES

How well did you spot story clues in this selection? Each of the following questions is based on a story clue found in Part 2 of the story. Each correct answer will help you solve the mystery of "The Speckled Band."

11. Holmes discovered that the bell rope

   a. was as old as the house.   *c.* worked perfectly.
   b. did not ring.

12. What was surprising about the ventilator?

   a. It was between two rooms.
   b. It reached the fresh air outside.
   c. It was very noisy.

13. Where was the ventilator located?

   a. next to the bell rope   *c.* near the door
   b. above the window

14. What did Holmes find on top of the safe?

   a. some business papers   *c.* a large cat
   b. a saucer of milk

15. What was unusual about the dog leash?

   a. It was long and brightly colored.
   b. It was locked in the safe.
   c. It was tied at the end in a small, tight loop.

Review your answers to the questions above. Keep these story clues in mind when you read the conclusion, or ending, to the story. You should be getting closer to solving the mystery of "The Speckled Band."

III. Finding Word Meanings

The ten words listed below appear in Part 2 of "The Adventure of the Speckled Band." Study the words and their definitions. Then complete the following paragraphs by using each vocabulary word only *once*. The first word has already been added.

		page
involved	interested in	15
detail	small part	17
active	lively; showing much attention	17
reflect	think carefully	18
furnished	supplied	18
satisfying	pleasing; enjoyable	19
positive	certain; sure	19
advice	opinion about what to do	19
investigation	a careful search	20
prefer	like better	20

To be a good reader, you must take an __16__ active part in the reading adventure. Learn to look for the story clues that the author has supplied, or __17__. Think carefully about each new item and __18__ in the story.

Reading, like detective work, requires __19__. Therefore, as you read, make it a habit to reason; to think and __20__. In a word, become more __21__ in what you are reading.

If you follow this __22__, we are __23__ that you will become a better reader. After a while you will __24__ to read this way. You will also find reading much more __25__.

IV. Reviewing the Case

Now it's time to review the case. Answer each of the following questions in a well-written paragraph.

A. Explain how Holmes examined the room in which Julia Stover had died. What did he find suspicious there?

B. At the end of the selection, Holmes states that he has a plan in mind. What do you think Holmes was planning? If you prefer, make up a plan of your own. Later, you may have an opportunity to share your answer with your classmates. It will be interesting to see whose plan comes closest to the one Holmes decided upon.

"Suddenly, the silence of the night was broken by a horrible scream. It was a hoarse yell filled with anger, pain and fear."

The Adventure of the Speckled Band

PART 3

Holmes and I had no trouble getting a room at the Crown Inn. It was on the top floor, and from our window we could easily see the old house at Stoke Moran. At dusk, we saw Dr. Grimesby Roylott drive up to the old house and open the door.

Holmes and I sat together waiting in the gathering darkness. "Do you know," he said after a while, "I really am quite concerned about your coming with me tonight. There may be some danger."

"Can I be of help?"

"Your assistance would be of the greatest value."

"Then I shall certainly come."

"That is very kind of you."

"You speak of danger, Holmes. Undoubtedly, you have seen more in those rooms than I did."

"No, but I believe I may have detected a little more."

"I saw nothing unusual except the bell rope. But what purpose that was for, I confess, I cannot imagine."

"You saw the ventilator, too," said Holmes.

"Yes, but I did not think it unusual to have a small open-

ing between two rooms. It was so small that a rat could hardly pass through it."

"I knew that we should find a ventilator before we ever came to Stoke Moran."

"And how could you know that, Holmes?"

"You will remember that Miss Stover's sister said she could smell Dr. Roylott's cigar. That suggested to me that there must be a common opening between the rooms. A ventilator came immediately to mind."

"But what importance can there be in that?"

"It is very curious, Watson. A ventilator is made, a bell cord is hung, and a lady who sleeps in the bed near them dies. Does anything strike you about that?"

"At the moment, I cannot see any connection."

"Did you observe anything peculiar about that bed?"

"No."

"It was nailed to the floor. Did you ever see a bed fastened like that before?"

"I cannot say that I have."

"The lady could not move her bed. It must therefore always be near the ventilator and the rope. I call it a rope for, clearly, it was never meant to be a bellpull."

"Holmes!" I cried. "I begin to see what you are hinting at. We are just in time to prevent another horrible crime!"

Now it's time for YOU to be The Reader as Detective

You have all the clues necessary for you to solve "The Adventure of the Speckled Band." Can you figure out how Julia Stover was murdered? Here are the clues:

- The dummy bell rope
- The ventilator
- The bed nailed to the floor
- The whistling sound
- The clanging sound
- Julia Stover's dying words
- The saucer of milk
- The safe
- The dog leash
- Dr. Roylott's love of animals from India

Read on to see if you are right!

At that moment, the lights in the old house at Stoke Moran went out and all was dark. Two hours passed slowly. Then, suddenly, at the stroke of eleven, a single bright light shone out from the house.

"That is our signal!" exclaimed Holmes. "It is coming from the middle window."

A moment later, we were on the dark road heading toward the house. We had just slipped into the garden and were about to enter through the window. Suddenly, from out of a clump of bushes, there darted some wild and hideous figure. Throwing itself upon the grass, it ran wildly across the garden and into the darkness.

"Holmes," I whispered. "Did you see it? What was that?"

For the moment, Holmes was as startled as I. Then he

broke into a low laugh. "This is a strange household," he murmured. "That was the baboon."

I had forgotten the strange pets which the doctor kept. There was a cheetah, too, I remembered. And I hoped we might not find it leaping onto our shoulders. I confess that I felt easier when we climbed through the window and entered the bedroom.

Holmes quietly closed the shutters of the window. He moved the lamp to the table, and looked around the room. Everything was just the way we had seen it in the daytime. Holmes whispered very softly to me, "We must sit here without light. He would see it through the ventilator."

I nodded to show that I had heard.

"Do not fall asleep. Your life may depend on it. Have your pistol ready in case we should need it. I will sit on the side of the bed while you sit in that chair."

I took out my revolver and placed it on the corner of the table. Holmes had brought a long, thin cane with him. He placed it on the bed beside him. Near it he put a box of matches and the stump of a candle. Then he turned off the lamp.

I shall never forget those hours. The shutters completely cut off the light, and we waited in complete darkness. From outside, now and then, came the cry of a bird. And once, we heard a long cat-like yowl. This told us that the cheetah was wandering about. Far away we could hear the church clock striking the hours. Twelve struck, and one, and two, and three o'clock—and still we sat and waited silently for whatever might happen.

Suddenly, there was a brief gleam of light from the direction of the ventilator. It went out immediately. This was followed by a strong smell of burning oil and heated metal. Someone in the next room had lit a lantern. There was the soft sound of someone moving. Then all was silent once more.

For half an hour I sat listening carefully. Then suddenly I heard another sound—like that of a small jet of steam escaping from a kettle. The instant we heard it, Holmes jumped from the bed. He lit a match, grabbed his cane, and struck furiously at the bellpull.

"Do you see it, Watson!" he yelled. "Do you see it!"

But I saw nothing. I had heard a low, clear whistle. But I

could not tell what it was at which my friend struck so furiously. I could, however, see that Holmes's face was deadly pale and was filled with horror and disgust.

Holmes had stopped lashing with his cane and was looking up at the ventilator. Suddenly, the silence of the night was broken by a horrible scream. It was a hoarse yell filled with anger, pain, and fear. They say that down in the village, that cry woke the sleepers in their beds. It struck cold to our hearts, and I stood gazing at Holmes until the last echoes of the cry had died away.

"What can that mean?" I gasped.

"It means that it is all over," Holmes answered. "Take your pistol, Watson, and we will enter Dr. Roylott's room."

With a grave face, Holmes lit the lamp and led the way down the hall. He knocked twice on the chamber door, but received no reply. Then he turned the handle and entered. I followed at his heels, pistol in hand.

It was a strange sight which met our eyes. On the table stood a lantern. It threw a brilliant beam of light on the iron safe whose door was thrown open. Beside the table, on the wooden chair, sat Dr. Grimesby Roylott. Across his lap lay the dog leash which we had noticed earlier that day.

Dr. Roylott's chin was pointed upward. His unmoving eyes were staring at the corner of the ceiling. Twisted around his forehead was a yellow band with brownish speckles.

"The band! The speckled band!" whispered Holmes.

I took a step forward. At that moment, the strange headband around the doctor's head began to move. There rose the diamond-shaped head and puffy neck of a snake.

"It's a swamp adder!" cried Holmes. "The deadliest snake in India. Dr. Roylott has died within ten seconds of being bitten! Quickly! Let us get this creature back into its den. Then we can alert Miss Stover, and let the police know what has happened."

As he spoke, Holmes took the dog leash from the dead man's lap. Holmes slipped the noose around the snake's neck. Then, carrying it at arm's length, he thrust it into the safe and slammed shut the door.

Such are the facts of the death of Dr. Grimesby Roylott of

Stoke Moran. What I had not yet learned about the case was told to me by Holmes as we traveled home.

"It became clear," said Holmes to me in the cab, "that no one could enter the room from the window or the door. The floor and walls were solid, too. My attention was quickly drawn to the ventilator, and to the bell rope which hung down to the bed. I soon discovered that this was a dummy—and that the bed was nailed to the floor. This led me to suspect that the rope was there to provide a bridge—for something coming out of the ventilator hole and going down to the bed. The idea that it might be a snake came to me at once. And when I realized that the doctor had been obtaining animals from India, I felt sure I was on the right track."

Holmes shook his head sadly. "Dr. Roylott was both clever and cruel. He used the knowledge he had gained in India. He knew that the swamp adder's poison takes effect at once, and that it is one which cannot be discovered by any chemical test. Moreover, it was quite unlikely that anyone would notice the two tiny dark holes where the snake's fangs had struck.

"You will remember, of course, the whistling sound of which both sisters spoke. It was necessary for Dr. Roylott to call back the snake before it could be discovered in the morning light. Dr. Roylott had trained it, probably by using milk, to return to him when he whistled. He would put the snake through the ventilator late at night. He knew that it would crawl down the rope and land on the bed. It might or might not bite whoever was sleeping there. She might escape every night for a week. But sooner or later, she would become the snake's victim.

"I had come to these conclusions before I ever entered Dr. Roylott's room. A careful inspection of this chair showed me that he often stood on it. This was necessary, of course, to reach the ventilator. When I saw the safe, the saucer of milk, and the dog leash with the loop, I was certain I was right. The metallic clang heard by Miss Stover was the safe closing to keep the snake in.

"Having once made up my mind, I took steps to obtain proof. Together we waited silently in the dark. Finally, when we heard the snake hiss, I quickly lit a match and attacked it with a cane."

"With the result that you drove it back through the ventilator."

"Where it turned upon its master. Angered by my blows, it struck at the first person it saw."

Holmes paused for a moment. "I fear," said he, "that I am indirectly responsible for the death of Dr. Roylott."

"Consider the nature of the man," said I. "And do not let it weigh too heavily upon your conscience."

At that moment, the cab stopped in front of our rooms on Baker Street. "And so, my dear Watson," said Holmes, "thus ends the mysterious Adventure of the Speckled Band."

I. The Reader as Detective

Read each of the following questions. Then write the letter of the correct answer to each question. Remember, the symbol next to each question identifies the *kind* of reading skill that particular question helps you to develop.

1. Holmes was afraid that Watson would
   a. be in danger.
   b. help him very little.
   c. solve the case.

2. Why was the bed nailed to the floor?
   a. because it looked good there
   b. to make it easy to clean the room
   c. to keep it close to the ventilator

3. Holmes and Watson saw a hideous figure dash wildly across the garden. What is the meaning of the word *hideous*?
   a. tiny   *b.* slow   *c.* ugly

4. What did Holmes bring with him?
   a. a cane   *b.* a pistol   *c.* a rope

5. Which happened last?
   a. Holmes and Watson waited at the inn.
   b. The snake bit Dr. Roylott.
   c. Watson heard a low, clear whistle.

6. "The band! The speckled band!" whispered Holmes."
What was Holmes speaking about?

    a. a band of vagabonds
    b. something worn around the head
    c. a snake

7. Which sentence expresses an opinion?

    a. "I fear," said Holmes, "that I am indirectly responsible for the death of Dr. Roylott."
    b. Holmes quietly closed the shutters of the window.
    c. Then suddenly, at the stroke of eleven, a single bright light shone out from the house.

8. "With a grave face, Holmes lit the lamp and led the way down the hall." As used in this sentence, which word or expression means the same as *grave*?

    a. serious   *c.* hole in the ground
    b. smiling

9. What is true of the swamp adder's poison?

    a. It is not very deadly.
    b. It takes effect after several hours.
    c. It takes effect at once.

10. Which sentence best tells what the story is mainly about?

    a. Dr. Roylott receives the punishment he deserves.
    b. Holmes solves the mystery of "The Speckled Band."
    c. Helen Stover gives a signal to Holmes and Watson.

II. On the Trail

DRAWING CONCLUSIONS

A good reader *draws conclusions*. These conclusions are based on facts and story clues found in the selection. As the reader as detective, you must learn to draw conclusions. The following questions will help you practice this skill.

11. Julia Stover was killed by

    a. her sister.   *c.* a snake.
    b. a cougar or a cheetah.

12. Why was the ventilator added to the room?

    a. to give the house a modern look
    b. to give the room fresh air
    c. to let the swamp adder pass through

13. The bell rope served as a kind of

    a. ladder.   *b.* signal.   *c.* whistle.

14. We may conclude that snakes

    a. come from India.
    b. are very small.
    c. like milk.

15. Dr. Roylott planned Helen's death because

    a. she was planning to be married.
    b. she had told her story to Sherlock Holmes.
    c. he had always hated her.

Review the answers to the questions above. How many of these conclusions had you already reached while you were reading the story? Your teacher may wish you to share and discuss these conclusions with your classmates.

III. Finding Word Meanings

The ten words listed below appear in Part 3 of "The Adventure of the Speckled Band." Study the words and their definitions. Then complete the following paragraphs by using each vocabulary word only *once*.

		page
assistance	help	25
connection	joining together	26
peculiar	strange	26
prevent	stop; keep from happening	27
brilliant	very bright	29
provide	offer up; supply	30
obtaining	getting	30
victim	a person injured or badly treated	30
conclusions	opinions reached through reasoning	30
inspection	the act of looking at closely	30

Sherlock Holmes undertook a careful __16__ of the rooms at Stoke Moran. He was searching for anything odd or __17__ . Nothing escaped the __18__ detective's sharp eyes.

Holmes was interested in just one thing—__19__ clues. Clues, Holmes knew that clues would __20__ the answer to what had happened to Julia Stover. Clues would provide the bridge, or __21__ , to who or what had been responsible for her death. They would lend __22__ to Holmes in his task. This was to __23__ the murderer from claiming another __24__ . Clues would help Holmes draw __25__ about the mystery he was trying to solve.

IV. Reviewing the Case

Now it's time to review the case. In a sentence or two explain how each of the following clues listed on pages 26–27 plays an important part in "The Adventure of the Speckled Band."

A. The dummy bell rope
B. The ventilator
C. The bed nailed to the floor
D. The whistling sound
E. The clanging sound
F. Julia Stover's dying words
G. The saucer of milk
H. The safe
I. The dog leash
J. Dr. Roylott's love of animals from India

After Twenty Years

by O. Henry

The policeman on the beat moved up the avenue slowly. The time was nearly ten o'clock at night, but the streets were almost empty. Cold winds, with a threat of rain in them, had driven most people inside.

Trying doors as he went and twirling his club, he cast a watchful eye about. Now and then you might see the lights of an all-night luncheonette. But most of the doors belonged to business places that had been closed for many hours.

In the middle of a certain block, the policeman suddenly slowed his walk. In the doorway of a darkened hardware store stood a man with an unlighted cigar in his mouth. As the policeman walked up to him, the man spoke up quickly.

"It's all right, officer," he said. "I'm just waiting for a friend. It's a date we made twenty years ago."

The policeman stared at the man.

"Sounds a little funny to you, doesn't it?" said the man. "Well, I'll explain if you'd like to make certain it's on the level. About that long ago there used to be a restaurant where this store stands—'Big Joe' Brady's restaurant."

"Until five years ago," said the policeman. "It was torn down then."

The man in the doorway struck a match and lit his cigar. The light showed a pale, square-jawed face with sharp eyes and a vivid little white scar near his right eyebrow. The ends of his scarf were held together with a pin. In its center was a large diamond.

"Twenty years ago tonight," said the man, "I ate here at 'Big Joe' Brady's with Jimmy Wells, my best friend, and the greatest pal in the world. He and I were raised here in New York, just like two brothers. I was eighteen and Jimmy was twenty. The next morning I was to leave for the West to make my fortune. But you couldn't have dragged Jimmy out of New York. He thought it was the only place on earth. Well, we agreed that night that we would meet here again exactly twenty years from that date and time. We said we'd come— no matter how we were, or how far we had to travel. We figured that in twenty years each of us ought to have his future worked out and his reputation made, whatever they were going to be."

"It sounds pretty interesting," said the policeman. "Rather a long time between get-togethers, though, it seems to me. Haven't you heard from your friend since you left?"

"Well, yes, for a time we wrote," said the other. "But after a year or two we lost track of each other. You see, the West is a pretty big place, and I kept hopping around over it pretty lively. But I know Jimmy will meet me here if he's alive, for he always was the truest, most reliable old chap in the world. He'll never forget. I came a thousand miles to stand in this door tonight, and it's worth it if my old partner shows up."

The waiting man pulled out a handsome watch. Its hands were set with small diamonds.

"Three minutes to ten," he announced. "It was exactly ten o'clock when we parted here at the restaurant door."

"Did pretty well out West, didn't you?" asked the policeman.

"You bet! I hope Jimmy has done half as well. He was kind of a plodder, though, good fellow as he was. I've had to compete with some of the sharpest guys around to make my success. A man gets in a groove in New York. It takes the West to make him razor sharp."

The policeman twirled his club and took a step or two. "I'll be on my way. Hope your friend turns up all right. Going to call time on him sharp?"

"I should say not!" said the other. "I'll give him another half an hour at least. If Jimmy is alive on earth, he'll be here by that time. So long, officer."

"Good night," said the policeman, passing on along his beat, trying doors as he went.

There was now a light, cold rain falling, and the wind was blowing harder. The few people on the streets hurried quickly and silently along, their coat collars turned high, their hands in their pockets. And in the door of the hardware store stood the man who had come a thousand miles to keep a date with the friend of his youth. He smoked his cigar and waited.

About twenty minutes he waited. Then a tall man in a long overcoat with the collar turned up to his ears hurried across from the other side of the street. He went straight to the waiting man.

"Is that you, Bob?" he asked, uncertainly.

"Is that you, Jimmy Wells?" cried the man in the door.

"Bless my heart!" exclaimed the man who had just arrived. He grabbed the other man's hands with his own. "It's Bob, sure as fate. I was sure I'd find you here if you were still alive. Well, well, well!—twenty years is a long time. The old restaurant's gone, Bob. I wish it had lasted, so we could have another dinner there. How has the West treated you, old man?"

"Great. It has granted me everything I asked it for. Say, you've changed lots, Jimmy. You're two or three inches taller than I remembered."

"Oh, I grew a few inches after I was twenty."

"Doing well in New York, Jimmy?"

"Pretty well. I have a position in one of the city's departments. Come on, Bob. We'll go to a place I know of, and have a good long talk about old times."

The two men started up the street, arm in arm. The man from the West, pleased with his success, was talking about himself. The other, huddled in his overcoat, listened with interest.

At the corner stood a drugstore, bright with lights. When they came into this glare, each of them turned at the same moment to gaze upon the other's face.

The man from the West stopped suddenly and let go of the other man's arm.

"You're not Jimmy Wells!" he snapped. "Twenty years is a long time—but not long enough to change the shape of a man's nose."

"It sometimes changes a good man into a bad one," said the tall man. "You've been under arrest for ten minutes, 'Silky' Bob. We got word from Chicago that you were heading our way. They want to have a little talk with you. Going quietly, are you? That makes sense. Now before we go to the station, here's a note I was asked to hand to you. You may read it here at the window. It's from Patrolman Wells."

The man from the West unfolded the little piece of paper that was handed to him. His hand was steady when he began to read it. But it trembled a little by the time he had finished. The note was rather short.

Now it's time for YOU to be The Reader as Detective.

What do you think Patrolman Wells's note said? Read on to see if you are right!

Bob: I was at the meeting place on time. When you struck the match to light your cigar, I saw it was the face of the man wanted in Chicago. Somehow I couldn't do it myself, so I went and got a plainclothesman to do the job.

Jimmy

I. The Reader as Detective

Read each of the following questions. Then write the letter of the correct answer to each question. Remember, the symbol next to each question identifies the *kind* of reading skill that particular question helps you to develop.

1. Which of the following best expresses the main idea of the story?
   a. People never change.
   b. A policeman places loyalty to duty over loyalty to friendship.
   c. One should never trust old friends.

2. The man from the West had
   a. a pale face with sharp eyes.   *c.* both of the above.
   b. a scar near his eyebrow.

3. "Silky" Bob was wearing
   a. a long overcoat with the collar turned up.
   b. expensive jewelry.   *c.* an old jacket.

4. We may infer that Jimmy Wells
   a. was unhappy about being a policeman.
   b. hated "Silky" Bob.
   c. was sorry to have his friend arrested.

5. Bob thought that Jimmy was "the truest, most reliable old chap in the world." Which word or expression best defines the word *reliable*?

   a. wealthy   *c.* long forgotten
   b. worthy of trust

6. What happened last in the story?

   a. The plainclothesman gave "Silky" Bob a letter.
   b. The policeman twirled his club and went on his way.
   c. Bob left for the West to make his fortune.

7. We may infer that Jimmy asked Bob how long he would wait for his friend because Jimmy

   a. was getting cold.
   b. wasn't sure the man was "Silky" Bob.
   c. wanted to make certain that Bob would wait there.

8. Which one of the following best describes the evening?

   a. bright and clear
   b. warm and pleasant
   c. cold and dark

9. "When they came into this glare, each of them turned at the same moment to gaze upon the other's face." As used in this sentence, the word *glare* means

   a. stare at.   *c.* anger.
   b. light.

10. Which one of the following is an opinion?

   a. Bob and Jimmy were once the best of friends.
   b. Jimmy arrived at the meeting place on time.
   c. "Silky" Bob was probably angry at Jimmy for turning him in.

II. On the Trail

STORY CLUES

   O. Henry, the author of "After Twenty Years," is famous for his "surprise" endings. However, his stories usually contain *clues* which suggest how the story will end. A careful reader can learn to *detect*, or spot, these clues and many guess how the story will end.

How good a reading detective are you? Did you spot some clues to the "surprise" ending in the story? Answer the questions below. They will give you practice in discovering clues in a story.

11. The man in the overcoat told Bob: "Oh, I grew a few inches after I was twenty." This is a clue that the man was not Jimmy Wells because
   a. Jimmy Wells was still out West.
   b. the man in the overcoat was taller than Jimmy.
   c. it is unusual for someone to grow a few inches after the age of twenty.

12. The man in the overcoat told Bob: "I have a position in one of the city's departments." This was true. For what department did he work?
   a. the police department
   b. the housing department
   c. the department of transportation

13. The new arrival stayed "huddled in his overcoat" with the "collar turned up to his ears." Why?
   a. He thought he looked good that way.
   b. He didn't want "Silky" Bob to see his face.
   c. He was wearing someone else's coat.

14. Although it was very dark, the man in the overcoat "hurried across from the other side of the street" and "went straight to the waiting man." This suggests that the man in the overcoat
   a. wasn't sure who the other man was.
   b. already knew who the other man was.
   c. didn't want to meet his old friend.

15. The author describes the waiting man as "razor sharp" with a "white scar near his right eyebrow." He also has a large diamond scarf pin and a handsome watch set with diamonds. Possibly, this is O. Henry's way of suggesting that the man
   a. has become wealthy in ways that are not honest.
   b. is not as rich as he appears to be.
   c. is quiet and shy although he is wealthy.

III. Finding Word Meanings

Listed below are five vocabulary words which appear in "After Twenty Years" and five *new* vocabulary words for you to learn. Study the words and their definitions. Then complete the following paragraphs by using each vocabulary word only *once*.

		page
vivid	lively; clear; distinct	36
reputation	good name; fame	36
compete	try to win something wanted by others	36
granted	given; awarded	37
steady	changing little; firm	38
beloved	dearly loved	
descriptions	pictures in words	
style	quality	
produced	brought forth	
numerous	many	

O. Henry is one of America's most __16__ short story writers. He gained his __17__, or fame, through the use of the "unexpected" or "surprise" ending. This gives his work so special a __18__, or manner of expression, that readers usually recognize it.

From 1900 to 1910, O. Henry wrote a __19__ stream of short stories. He __20__ about 600 in all.

O. Henry loved New York City. It is the setting he chose for many, or __21__, stories. These stories contain characters who are lively, __22__, and distinct, along with striking scenes and excellent __23__ of big-city life.

Today, writers __24__ for a prize called the O. Henry Award. It is __25__ for the best American short story written each year.

IV. Reviewing the Case

Now it's time to review the case. "After Twenty Years" ends with a note from Jimmy to Bob. Suppose Bob could answer Jimmy's note. What do you think he would say? Write a brief note from Bob to Jimmy. Try not to have Bob express anger in his answer. First make a rough copy of the note. Then proofread and correct it. Afterwards, write your final copy.

The Open Window

by Saki

"My aunt will be down in a few minutes, Mr. Nuttel," said a very calm young lady of fifteen. "But for now, you must try to put up with me."

Framton Nuttel looked at the young lady. He tried to think of something polite to say to her. But he was very nervous. In fact, he had come to the country as a cure for his nerves. And talking to strangers only got him more upset.

"I know how it will be," Framton's sister had said, when he was getting ready to leave. "You will stay by yourself down there in the country. You won't say a word to a living soul. Then your nerves will be worse than ever. Look, I'll give you the names of people I met there. Some of them, I remember, seemed quite nice."

Framton wondered if Mrs. Sappleton was one of the "nice" ones.

Several moments of silence passed. Then the young lady's voice broke the silence. "Do you know many people around here?" she asked.

"Hardly a soul," said Framton. "My sister lived in this area four years ago. She gave me a letter of introduction to Mrs. Sappleton."

"Then you know almost nothing about my aunt?" asked the calm young lady.

"Only her name and address," admitted Framton.

He was wondering if Mrs. Sappleton was married. Something about the room seemed to suggest that a man lived there.

"Her great tragedy happened just three years ago," said the girl. "That was after your sister left."

"Her tragedy?" asked Framton. Somehow in this restful country spot tragedies seemed out of place.

"You may wonder why we keep that window wide open on an October afternoon," said the niece. She pointed to a large French window that opened onto the lawn.

"It is quite warm for this time of year," said Framton. "But has that window got anything to do with the tragedy?"

"Out through that window, exactly three years ago today, her husband and her two brothers went off hunting. They never came back. They were drowned, all three. It had been that terribly wet summer, you know. Places that were safe in other years gave way suddenly without warning. Their bodies were never found. That was the worst part of it."

Here, for the first time, the girl's voice became less calm. It began to crack. "Poor dear aunt always thinks that they will come back some day. They and the little brown dog that was lost with them. She believes that they will walk through that window, just as they used to. That is why the window is always kept open until dark."

The girl paused and shook her head sadly. "Poor dear aunt. She has often told me how they went out. Her husband had his raincoat over his arm. Ronnie, her younger brother, was singing 'It's a long way to Tipperary.' He always did that to tease her. She said it got on her nerves. Do you know, sometimes, on still, quiet evenings like this, I almost get a creepy feeling that they will all walk in through that window . . . ."

She broke off with a little shudder. It was a relief to Framton when the aunt burst into the room. She apologized for being so late.

"I hope Vera has been amusing you," she said.

"She has been very . . . interesting," said Framton.

"I hope you don't mind the open window," said Mrs. Sappleton brightly. "My husband and brothers will be home soon

from hunting. They always come in that way. They've been out in the marsh, so they'll certainly mess up my poor carpets. So like you menfolk, isn't it?"

She chatted cheerfully about hunting. She went on about how few birds there were that season, and how to find ducks in the winter. It was horrible to Framton. He tried again and again, without success, to change the subject. But Mrs. Sappleton was hardly listening to him. Her eyes kept looking past him to the open window and the lawn beyond. It certainly was unlucky that he should have come visiting just three years to the day when her family was lost.

"The doctors agree that I must have complete rest," said Framton. "I must not have any kind of excitement at all. On the matter of my diet, they are really not sure."

"No?" said Mrs. Sappleton, holding back a yawn. But suddenly she brightened into alert attention—but not at what Framton was saying.

"Here they are at last!" she cried. "Just in time for tea. And don't they look muddy up to their eyes!"

Framton shivered slightly and turned to give the girl a knowing look. But the girl was staring out through the open window. There was a look of dazed horror in her eyes. In a chill shock of nameless fear, Framton swung round in his seat. He looked in the same direction.

In the darkening twilight, three figures were walking across the lawn towards the window. They all carried guns under their arms. One of them had a raincoat thrown over his shoulder. A tired brown dog kept close at their heels. Quietly they neared the house. Then a deep young voice sang out, "It's a long way to Tipperary!"

Framton jumped out of his chair. He wildly grabbed his hat. Within seconds he had raced down the hall, up the road, and through the front gate. A man riding a bicycle had to drive into the bushes to avoid an accident.

"Here we are, my dear," said the man with the raincoat. "It's a bit muddy out, but most of it's dry. Who was that who dashed out as we came up?"

"A very strange man, a Mr. Nuttel," said Mrs. Sappleton. "He could talk only about how ill he was, and bolted off without a word when you arrived. One would think he had seen a ghost."

Now it's time for YOU to be The Reader as Detective.

What do you think Vera answered? What do you think she might have said?
Read on to see if you are right!

"It probably was our dog," said Vera calmly. "He told me he had a terrible fear of dogs. Once, in India, he was chased into a cemetery by a pack of wild dogs. He had to spend the night in a newly dug grave, with the creatures barking and snarling just above him. That would make anyone nervous."

Vera loved to make up stories on the spot. She was really quite good at it.

I. The Reader as Detective

Read each of the following questions. Then write the letter of the correct answer to each question. Remember, the symbol next to each question identifies the *kind* of reading skill that particular question helps you to develop.

1. Framton had come to the country to

   a. enjoy nature.   *c.* cure his nerves.

   b. visit his sister.

2. We may infer that Mrs. Sappleton's husband and brothers

   a. were drowned while hunting.

   b. were never lost at all.

   c. returned after several years.

3. Framton's sister gave him

   a. a letter of introduction.   *c.* a house to live in.

   b. a cup of tea.

4. The aunt burst into the room and apologized for being so late. What is the meaning of the word *apologize*?

   a. to be angry   *c.* to speak loudly

   b. to say one is sorry

5. Which happened last?

   a. Mrs. Sappleton chatted cheerfully about hunting.

   b. Framton explained that he needed complete rest.

   c. Vera stared in horror through the open window.

6. Which of the following is a fact?

   a. After leaving the Sappleton's home, Framton went straight to his doctor.

   b. Vera probably hoped that Framton would visit again.

   c. Mrs. Sappleton hardly listened to Framton.

7. At the end of the story, Framton probably thought that

   a. he was seeing ghosts.

   b. Vera had been lying to him.

   c. Mrs. Sappleton was surprised to see her family.

8. Mrs. Sappleton stated that Framton had "bolted off without a word." As used in this sentence, what is the meaning of the word *bolted*?

   a. fastened   *b.* nailed   *c.* raced

9. According to Vera, when had the "great tragedy" happened?

   a. three years ago   *c.* 15 years ago

   b. four years ago

10. Which sentence best expresses the main idea of the story?

   a. Three men return home from hunting.

   b. A young storyteller strikes again.

   c. Framton Nuttel has a terrible fear of dogs.

II. On the Trail

DISCERNING CHARACTER

To fully enjoy and appreciate what you are reading, you must learn to recognize, or *discern*, character. In "The Open Window," for example, Framton's character—the kind of person he is—plays an important part in the story.

As the reader as detective, you must discern character. The following questions will help you practice this skill.

11. Which group of words best describes Framton Nuttel?

   a. witty and charming
   b. nervous and uncomfortable
   c. friendly and amusing

12. Which sentence best characterizes Vera?

   a. She was quite dull.
   b. She was very shy.
   c. She had a lively imagination.

13. Mrs. Sappleton thought that Framton was

   a. rather boring and strange.
   b. very interesting.
   c. in excellent health.

14. Which one of the following is true of Vera?

   a. She was a very fine actress.
   b. She was afraid of strangers.
   c. She hated telling stories.

15. When Framton saw the hunters, he found it especially shocking because

   a. he was easily excited.
   b. he needed quiet and rest.
   c. both of the above.

III. Finding Word Meanings

Following are five vocabulary words which appear in "The Open Window" and five *new* vocabulary words for you to learn. Study the words and their definitions. Then complete the following paragraphs by using each vocabulary word only *once*.

		page
introduction	beginning or starting point; making known	43
tragedy	a terrible happening; unusual sadness	44
shudder	shake with fear	44

page

alert	wide-awake; very watchful	46
chill	make cold; sudden coldness	46
construct	put together; build	
attempt	make an effort; try	
typical	of a type; a good example	
similar	alike; much the same	
innocent	doing no harm; simple	

"The Open Window" is a good beginning, or __16__, to the tales of Saki. The story is __17__ of his work. It begins in a very __18__, simple manner. But its conclusion may make you either __19__ or laugh.

Some of Saki's stories are very amusing. Others, however, end on a note of __20__. These stories can __21__ you to the bone.

Saki and O. Henry are very __22__ in style. Both authors __23__ to surprise their readers. They __24__ the endings to their stories with this in mind. Therefore, be especially __25__ when you read their works.

IV. Reviewing the Case

Now it's time to review the case.

A. Vera asked, "Then you know almost nothing about my aunt?" "Only her name and address," admitted Framton. In two or three sentences, explain why you think Vera asked this question, and why the information she received was so important.

B. Suppose Framton Nuttel wrote a letter to his sister telling about his visit to Mrs. Sappleton's home. What do you think he would say? Pretend you are Framton Nuttel. Write a letter to "Dear Sister," describing your visit. First make a rough draft of your letter. Make corrections. Then write your final draft. Later, you and your classmates may have the opportunity to exchange letters. Which ones did you like best? Why?

"I want to know just what control everyone at this table has. I will count three hundred—that's five minutes—and not one of you is to move a muscle."

The Dinner Party

by Mona Gardner

The country is India. A colonial official and his wife are giving a large dinner party. They are seated with their guests—army officers and government attachés and their wives, and a visiting American naturalist—in their spacious dining room, which has a bare marble floor, open rafters, and wide glass doors opening onto a veranda.

A spirited discussion springs up between a young girl who insists that women have outgrown the jumping-on-a-chair-at-the-sight-of-a-mouse era and a colonel who says that they haven't.

"A woman's unfailing reaction in any crisis," the colonel says, "is to scream. And while a man may feel like it, he has that ounce more of nerve control than a woman has. And that last ounce is what counts."

The American does not join in the argument but watches the other guests. As he looks, he sees a strange expression come over the face of the hostess. She is staring straight ahead, her muscles contracting slightly. With a slight gesture, she summons the native boy standing behind her chair and whispers to him. The boy's eyes widen, and he quickly leaves the room.

Of the guests, none except the American notices this or sees the boy place a bowl of milk on the veranda just outside the open doors.

The American comes to with a start. In India, milk in a bowl means only one thing—bait for a snake. He realizes there must be a cobra in the room. He looks up at the rafters—the likeliest place—but they are bare. Three corners of the room are empty, and in the fourth the servants are waiting to serve the next course. There is only one place left—under the table.

His first impulse is to jump back and warn the others, but he knows the commotion would frighten the cobra into striking. He speaks quickly, the tone of his voice so arresting that it sobers everyone.

"I want to know just what control everyone at this table has. I will count three hundred—that's five minutes—and not one of you is to move a muscle. Those who move will forfeit fifty rupees. Ready!"

The twenty people sit like stone images while he counts. He is saying ". . . two hundred and eighty . . ." when, out of the corner of his eye, he sees the cobra emerge and make for the bowl of milk. Screams ring out as he jumps to slam the veranda doors safely shut.

"You were right, Colonel!" the host exclaims. "A man has just shown us an example of perfect control."

"Just a minute," the American says, turning to his hostess. "Mrs. Wynnes, how did you know that cobra was in the room?"

> Now it's time for YOU to be The Reader as Detective.
>
> What do you think Mrs. Wynnes answered? Read on to see if you are right.

A faint smile lights up the woman's face as she replies: "Because it was crawling across my foot."

I. The Reader as Detective

Read each of the following questions. Then write the letter of the correct answer to each question. Remember, the symbol next to each question identifies the *kind* of reading skill that particular question helps you to develop.

1. "The Dinner Party" takes place in

    a. America.   *b.* India.   *c.* England.

2. Which happened first?

    a. A strange look came over the face of the hostess.
    b. The American began to count to three hundred.
    c. A young girl and a colonel began to argue.

3. The room contained "wide glass doors opening onto a veranda." What is a *veranda*?

    a. a porch   *b.* a floor   *c.* a roof

4. Mrs. Wynnes knew that the cobra was in the room because

    a. she saw it.   *c.* it was crawling across her foot.
    b. it was a pet.

5. "The Dinner Party" makes the point that

    a. men have more nerve than women do.
    b. a woman may have as much nerve as a man.
    c. women usually jump on a chair at the sight of a mouse.

6. The cobra headed for

    a. the rafters.
    b. a corner of the room.
    c. the bowl.

7. The American was afraid that "the commotion would frighten the cobra into striking." Which of the following best defines the word *commotion*?

    a. a sudden, noisy, moving about
    b. soft music
    c. a large crowd

8. Which sentence does *not* express an opinion?

    a. Women have more nerve than men do.
    b. Men have more nerve than women do.
    c. In India, milk is used as bait for cobras.

9. The American stated that anyone who moved would "forfeit fifty rupees." What is the meaning of the word *forfeit*?

    a. win   *b.* lose   *c.* find

10. Suppose this story appeared as a newspaper article. Which of the following would make the best headline?

    a. Large Dinner Party Given by the Wynneses
    b. Event at Dinner Party Proves Colonel Wrong
    c. American Sees Strange Look on Mrs. Wynnes's Face

II. On the Trail

DISCERNING CHARACTER

As you know, to fully enjoy and appreciate what you are reading, you must learn to recognize, or *discern*, character. In "The Dinner Party,'' for example, the words and actions of the characters play a very important part in the story.

As reader as detective, you must recognize characterization. The following questions will help you practice this skill.

11. The colonel believed that

    a. women handle difficult situations better than men do.

    b. men handle difficult situations better than women do.

    c. women and men handle difficult situations equally well.

12. Mrs. Wynnes's actions showed that she

    a. could control her emotions very well.

    b. usually became frightened easily.

    c. could not think quickly in an emergency.

13. The young girl believed that women

    a. jump on chairs at the sight of a mouse.

    b. prefer to live in the past.

    c. do not wish to be thought of as helpless.

14. Select the pair of words that best describes Mrs. Wynnes.

    a. brave, calm

    b. weak, nervous

    c. smart, frightened

15. The American's plan was to

    a. scare the cobra and then kill it.

    b. keep everyone quiet until the cobra came out.

    c. have everyone rush out of the room.

III. Finding Word Meanings

The following ten words appear in ''The Dinner Party.'' Study the words and their definitions. Then complete the following paragraphs by using each vocabulary word only *once*.

		page
spacious	containing much space; large	51
discussion	a talk between two or more people	51
reaction	an answer, by word or deed, to some action	51

		page
crisis	a very difficult or important event or time	51
control	hold back; have power over	51
argument	a talk, or discussion, by people who do not agree with each other	51
hostess	a woman who receives another person or other persons as her guest(s)	51
tone	manner of speaking or writing	52
arresting	very striking; holding one's attention	52
emerge	come out; come into view	52

"The Dinner Party" is set in a __16__ dining room. There, two guests are discussing a question. Soon their calm __17__ turns into an __18__ . It is about how well women can __19__ their emotions during a moment of excitement or __20__ . At the end of the story, the response, or __21__ , of the __22__ , Mrs. Wynnes, proves that one of the guests is correct.

There is something __23__ about "The Dinner Party" and "The Adventure of the Speckled Band." The stories are different in __24__ . But the ending of each story has something in common. In both, a snake manages to __25__ . Milk for the snake is also important in each story.

IV. Reviewing the Case

Now it's time to review the case. Think about how Mrs. Wynnes acted in "The Dinner Party." Then think about Framton Nuttel in "The Open Window." In a paragraph or two, *compare* Mrs. Wynnes and Mr. Nuttel. A brief outline may assist you in answering the question. Fold a sheet of paper in half. Label one side, "Mrs. Wynnes." Label the other side, "Mr. Nuttel." Write a few important facts about each. Refer to these as you write your answer.

The Purloined Letter

PART 1

by Edgar Allan Poe

In Paris, one windy evening, I was visiting my good friend, the world-famous detective, C. Auguste Dupin. Our conversation was interrupted by a loud knocking on the door. Dupin threw it open. There stood Mr. Gerrard, the Chief of the Paris Police.

We gave him a hearty welcome, for he was a delightful old friend whom we had not seen for many years.

"I am sorry to trouble you," said Gerrard. Here he turned to Dupin. "But I would like to ask your opinion about a recent case. It has been causing me a great deal of trouble."

"Please have a seat," said Dupin. He pointed to a comfortable chair.

"The fact is," said the Chief, "the case is very simple, very simple indeed. And yet, it is very odd."

"Simple and odd," said Dupin.

"Why, yes," said the Chief. "The truth is, we have all been quite puzzled because the case *is* so simple. But we can't figure it out."

"Perhaps it is *too* simple," said my friend.

"What nonsense you talk," replied the Chief. He burst into laughter.

"Perhaps the mystery is a little *too* plain," said Dupin.

"Oh, good heavens! Who ever heard of such an idea?"

"Perhaps it is a little too obvious."

"Ha! ha! ha!" roared our visitor. "Oh, Dupin, you will be the death of me yet."

"What is the case about?" I asked.

"I will tell you," replied the Chief. "But before I begin, let me caution you. The case is highly secret. I would probably lose my position if it became known that I discussed it with anyone."

"Begin," said I.

"Or not," said Dupin.

"Well then," said the Chief, "I have received information. It comes from a highly placed person in the government. I have learned that something of the greatest importance has been purloined—yes, *stolen*—from an office in the royal palace."

We stared at the Chief without saying a word.

"We know who stole it," the Chief went on. "The man was seen taking it. It is also known that he has it still."

"And what is the name of the thief?" asked Dupin.

The Chief lowered his voice. "The thief," he said, "is one of the most important and powerful ministers in the government. It is the Minister Darion."

"And what has been stolen?" I asked.

"The thing in question," said the Chief, "is a letter. It is a letter which is immensely valuable because it could prove quite embarrassing to the government. It is therefore very important that we get it back as quickly as possible."

The Chief paused. "And the responsibility for that has fallen to me."

"I can imagine," said Dupin, "no abler person for such a task."

"Thank you," said the Chief of Police.

"You are certain," said I, "that the Minister still has the letter."

"Of that we are certain," said the Chief. "My first move, therefore, was to search the Minister's house. The problem lay in the need to search it without his finding this out. I had been warned of the danger which would result from giving him reason to suspect our plan."

"But," I said, "you are experienced in doing these things."

"Oh, yes," said he. "And therefore I was not very worried. Besides, the habits of the Minister gave me an advantage. He is often away from his home all night. He has just two servants, and they do not sleep in the house."

The Chief took a deep breath before continuing. "I have keys, as you know, with which I can open any door in Paris. For many nights, I secretly searched the Minister's house. My reputation is at stake. And, to mention a secret—the reward is enormous. So I did not stop searching until I had looked everywhere. I tell you, I looked through every corner and crack of that house. I looked every place where it is possible that letter could be hidden. And yet I found nothing!"

"But is it not possible," I asked, "that the Minister has hidden the letter outside the house?"

"That is not possible," said Dupin. "It would be too dangerous. Besides, he is watched all the time."

"Then," I stated, "the letter must still be in the house. As for its being upon the person of the Minister, is that out of the question?"

"Completely," said the Chief. "Twice I arranged to have him robbed. He was carefully searched. Nothing was found."

"You might have saved yourself the trouble." said Dupin. "The Minister is hardly a fool. He must have known that might happen."

"Suppose you tell us," I said, "exactly how you searched his home."

"Why," said the Chief, "the fact is, we took our time. We searched *everywhere*. I went over the entire house, room by room. First we examined the furniture in each room. We opened every drawer. And I think you know, that to a well-trained police officer, such a thing as a 'secret' drawer is impossible. Next we looked at the chairs. The cushions we checked with the thin, metal needles you have seen me use.

Then we removed the tops from the tables."

"Why?" I asked.

"The top of a table—or other piece of furniture—is some-times removed by someone who wishes to conceal something. The person drills a hole into the leg. The thing is put into the hole. Then the top is put back on. The tops and bottoms of bedposts are often used this way."

"But you could not have taken apart *all* the pieces of fur-niture into which a letter might have been slipped. After all, a letter may be wound into a long, thin roll."

"Certainly not. But we did even better. We brought a very powerful microscope. With it we carefully examined the wood on every piece of furniture in the house. Had there been any recent change, we would have spotted it at once. A few grains of dust would have looked as large as apples. Any change in the glue would immediately have been seen."

"I suppose you checked the mirrors. And the beds and the bedclothes, the curtains and carpets."

"Of course. And when we had finished examining every-thing in the house, then we looked at the house itself. We di-vided its entire surface into sections. We numbered each one so that none might be missed. Then we checked every square inch with our microscope."

"You went to a great deal of trouble," I said.

"I did. But the reward that was offered is huge."

"Did you look at the grounds around the house?"

"All the grounds are covered with brick. They gave us very little trouble. We looked at the moss between the bricks and found it untouched."

"You looked among the Minister's papers, of course. And into the books in the library?"

"Certainly. We opened every book; we turned over every page in each volume. And we carefully checked the covers and backing."

"You explored the floors beneath the carpets?"

"Beyond doubt. We removed every carpet. Then we ex-amined the boards with the microscope."

"And the paper on the walls?"

"Yes."

"You looked in the cellar?"

"We did."

"Then," I said, "you are mistaken. The letter is *not* in the house, as you think."

"I am afraid you are right," said the Chief. He turned to Dupin. "And now, Dupin," he asked, "what do you suggest I do?"

"Search the house again."

"But that would serve no point," said the Chief. "As sure as I am breathing, that letter is not in the house."

"I have no better advice to give you," said Dupin.

He looked closely at the Chief. "You have an accurate description of the letter, of course."

"Oh, yes," said the Chief. Here he took out a notebook. Slowly, he began to read a careful description of the letter. Soon afterwards, he left. He seemed far sadder than I had ever seen the good gentleman before.

About a month later, the Chief paid us another visit. I could hardly wait to speak to him. "Well," I asked, "what of the stolen letter?"

"As Dupin suggested, I searched the house again. But as I expected, nothing turned up."

"How much is the reward?" asked Dupin, slowly.

"Why, a very great deal—a great deal, indeed. I don't want to say exactly. But one thing I will tell you. I would gladly give a check for fifty thousand francs to anyone who could get me that letter."

"In that case," said Dupin, "you might as well write me a check for the amount you mentioned. And when you have signed it, I will hand you the letter."

I was astounded. The Chief appeared thunderstruck. For several moments, he remained speechless and stared at my friend.

Finally, he recovered. Grabbing a pen, he wrote a check for fifty thousand francs and handed it to Dupin. Dupin looked at the check carefully. Then, unlocking a drawer, he pulled out a letter and gave it to the Chief.

With a trembling hand, the Chief unfolded the letter. He cast a quick glance at the words. Then rushing to the door, the Chief dashed out.

When I had gotten over my surprise, I turned to Dupin. "Please explain," I said.

> Now it's time for YOU to be The Reader as Detective.
>
> How could Dupin know where the letter was hidden when the Chief and his men were unable to find it? Where do you think Dupin might have looked? Think about the hints in the story before you read Part 2.

I. The Reader as Detective

Read each of the following questions. Then write the letter of the correct answer to each question. Remember, the symbol next to each question identifies the *kind* of reading skill that particular question helps you to develop.

 1. Dupin thought that the case was

    a. too hard.   *c.* not very important.

    b. too simple.

 2. The letter was stolen from

    a. the royal palace.

    b. Gerrard's home.

    c. an office in the Paris police station.

 3. Which happened last?

    a. Gerrard searched the Minister's house.

    b. Dupin gave the Chief a letter.

    c. Gerrard gave Dupin a check.

 4. Dupin stated that "a letter may be wound into a long, thin roll." As used in this sentence, the word *wound* means

    a. broken.   *c.* a hurt or an injury.

    b. turned or twisted.

 5. What did the Chief use when he searched the house?

    a. a powerful microscope   *c.* both of the above

    b. metal needles

6. Which of the following quotations from the story expresses an opinion?

    a. "I can imagine," said Dupin, "no abler person than you for such a task."

    b. "He has just two servants, and they do not sleep in the house."

    c. "First we examined the furniture in each room."

7. We may infer that Dupin

    a. didn't know where the Minister lived.

    b. didn't think he would find the letter.

    c. went to the Minister's house.

8. Gerrard arranged to have the Minister

    a. beaten.

    b. robbed.

    c. given a reward.

9. The Chief explained that "We opened every book; we turned over every page in each volume." As used in this sentence, what is the meaning of the word *volume*?

    a. loudness   *b.* space   *c.* book

10. This selection tells mainly about

    a. the search for a stolen letter.

    b. the life of C. Auguste Dupin.

    c. the most powerful Minister in the government.

II. On the Trail

HINTS AND SUGGESTIONS

In a mystery story, the author usually provides *hints* and *suggestions* which help the reader find the solution. As the reader as detective, you must learn to recognize these hints.

The correct answer to each of the following questions offers a hint or suggestion to finding the stolen letter.

11. According to Dupin, the mystery was

    a. impossible to solve.   *c.* possibly a little too plain.

    b. very uninteresting.

12. Dupin and the Chief both agreed that

    a. the letter was not in the house.

    b. the letter was not on the person of the Minister.

    c. the Minister had the letter with him.

13. The Chief and the police searched

    a. some of the rooms of the house.

    b. just the grounds around the house.

    c. every possible hiding place.

14. Gerrard thought that the Minister hid the letter

    a. in a secret spot.   *c.* in an office in the palace.

    b. out in the open.

15. Dupin suggested that the Chief

    a. search the Minister again.

    b. search the house again.

    c. forget about finding the letter.

Review your answers to the questions above. Keep them in mind as you read Part 2 of "The Purloined Letter."

III. Finding Word Meanings

The ten words listed below appear in "The Purloined Letter," Part 1. Study the words and their definitions. Then complete the following paragraphs by using each vocabulary word only *once.*

		page
conversation	friendly talk	57
recent	done not long ago; not long past	57
obvious	easily seen or understood	58
caution	warning	58
purloined	stolen	58
immensely	very greatly	58
responsibility	a task or job that one is expected to do	58
conceal	hide; keep secret	61
accurate	without errors; correct	62
astounded	greatly surprised	62

Mr. Gerrard, the Chief of the Paris Police, had a __16__ with the famous detective, C. Auguste Dupin. The Chief said that he needed some advice about his newest, or most __17__ , case. He explained that it was his __18__ to find a letter which someone had stolen—a __19__ letter.

The Chief was shocked and __20__ at what Dupin suggested. The detective said, "Let me offer you a word of warning and __21__ . The answer to this mystery may be a little too clear and __22__ ."

Gerrard was __23__ amused at this suggestion. He could not believe that Dupin was correct, or __24__ . Unable to __25__ his feelings, Gerrard burst into laughter.

IV. Reviewing the Case

Now it's time to review the case. Suppose that Chief Gerrard wrote a police report describing his search for the hidden letter. What do you think the report would say? In 75 to 100 words, write Gerrard's report. Note: Before you write your report, make a list of the items you wish to include. Then number them in the order in which you think they should appear. Use this outline as a guide in writing your report.

The Purloined Letter

PART 2

Dupin settled into a chair. "The police of Paris," said he, "are very able. They are hardworking and smart, and they know their business. So when the Chief explained how they had searched the Minister's house, I felt sure that they had done it very well—as far as they went."

"As far as they went?"

"Yes," said Dupin. "Their methods were the best of their kind, and carried out perfectly. Had the letter been within range of their search, those fellows would certainly have found it."

I laughed. But Dupin seemed quite serious in all that he said.

"Yes," said Dupin, "their methods were quite wrong for the man and the case."

"Wrong?" said I.

"You see," said Dupin, "the Chief and his men consider only their *own* ideas of being clever. So in searching for anything hidden, they think of the ways in which *they* would have hidden it. Do you not see that the Chief believes that *all* men would hide a letter in a hole drilled in a chair—or under a floorboard, or in some out-of-the-way place. And had the letter been hidden in that kind of secret spot, they would surely have found it."

"But the Minister is a man of great intelligence. I felt sure he was aware of the methods to be used against him. He must have known that he himself would be robbed. He must have known that his home would be searched."

Dupin paused for a moment. "Yes," said he, "the Chief was delighted that the Minister so often stayed away from home all night. But I immediately saw this as a trick by the Minister. He purposely stayed away—to give the police plenty of time to carefully search the house. Thus they could convince themselves that the letter was not there."

"But what happened to the letter?"

"The Minister," said Dupin, "must have known how foolish it would be to hide it in any of the usual hiding spots. He must have known how every out-of-the-way space would be searched. I realized that he would be forced to do something *simple*. Remember how the Chief laughed when I first suggested that perhaps this mystery troubled him so much because it was so obvious."

"I remember it well. How loudly he laughed."

A smile crossed Dupin's face. He continued to smile. "But *what of* the letter?" I demanded.

> Now it's time for YOU to be The Reader as Detective.
>
> *What of* the letter? Where do you think the Minister "hid" it? Dupin's words should help you decide where to look. Read on to see if you are right—and to discover how Dupin succeeded in escaping with the letter.

"The Chief never once," Dupin went on, "thought it probable or possible that the Minister had deposited the letter beneath the nose of the whole world—as the best way of preventing the world from seeing it. Yes, the more I thought about it, the more convinced I became that to hide the letter, the Minister had decided on the excellent plan of not hiding it at all."

"With this idea in mind, I put on a pair of green glasses. Then I called at the Minister's home. Once in his study, I complained to him of my weak eyes because of which, I explained, I wore the glasses. Under their cover, I carefully looked around. All the while, I made believe I was very interested in what the Minister was saying.

"I paid keen attention to a large desk. On it were some letters, papers, a musical instrument, and a few books. I looked at them carefully and long. But I saw nothing to make me suspicious. I continued to look around the room. Finally, my eyes stopped on an old cardboard letter holder. It was hanging from a blue ribbon attached to a nail over the fireplace.

"The holder had three compartments. In them were five or six cards and a letter. The letter was soiled and crumpled, and was torn nearly in half across the middle. It looked as though someone had decided to tear it up and had then changed his mind. The letter was addressed to the Minister in small, clear handwriting. It seemed to have been thrown carelessly into one of the compartments of the rack.

"As soon as I saw this letter, I was sure it was the very one for which I was searching. It is true that it appeared quite different from the letter which the Chief had described to us. In that one, the handwriting was large, and the letter was addressed to a member of the government. Here the handwriting was small, and the letter was addressed to the Minister. Still, this letter was dirty and torn, unusual for a Minister so tidy and neat. And that it should be there, in the full view of every visitor—that made me suspicious.

"I stayed as long as possible. All the while, I kept talking about a subject that I knew the Minister found fascinating. But I kept staring at the letter. I set my mind to remembering exactly how it looked and its place in the rack. Finally, I made a discovery that convinced me I was right!"

"What was that?" I asked eagerly.

"In looking at the edges of the paper, I noticed them to be more broken than seemed necessary. It was as though the letter had been folded, and then folded again in the *opposite* direction. It was clear to me that the letter had been turned, as a glove, inside out, and had been addressed again. I said goodbye to the Minister and went out. But I made sure to leave my cigarette case on the table.

"The next morning I returned for the cigarette case. While the Minister and I were talking, we heard loud shots, and

shouts coming from outside. The Minister rushed to the window, threw it open and looked out. At that moment, I stepped to the letter holder. I quickly took the letter and put it into my pocket. I replaced it with another letter which looked exactly like the first.

"The problem outside had been caused by a man with a gun. He had been firing it at a crowd. However, it seems that he was only firing blanks, so they called the fellow a madman and let him go on his way. A few moments later, I left the Minister's house. The 'madman,' of course, was a man I had hired."

"Excellent!" I said. "Excellent! But why did you replace the letter with another that looked just like it? Wouldn't it have been better, at the first visit, to have grabbed the letter and run?"

"The Minister," said Dupin, "is an exceedingly dangerous man. His house is not without guards. Had I made the wild attempt you suggest, I might never have left him alive. The good people of Paris would have heard of me no more."

Dupin began to laugh. "I confess," he said, "I would very much like to be there when he opens the letter which I left in the letter rack."

"Why? Did you write anything special in it?"

"It did not seem right to leave the inside of the letter blank. So I just wrote in these words:

> *Your little plan was quite well done.*
> *But my plan was a better one.*"

I. The Reader as Detective

Read each of the following questions. Then write the letter of the correct answer to each question. Remember, the symbol next to each question identifies the *kind* of reading skill that particular question helps you to develop.

1. Before Dupin went to the Minister's house, he put on

    a. a pair of green gloves.   *c.* a dark suit.
    b. a pair of green glasses.

2. Where did the Minister "hide" the letter?

    a. under a floorboard
    b. in a hole drilled in a chair
    c. in a cardboard letter holder

3. Which happened last?

    a. The Minister rushed to the window and threw it open.
    b. Dupin complained about his weak eyes.
    c. Dupin quickly took the letter and put it into his pocket.

4. The man with the gun

    a. was crazy.
    b. had been hired by Dupin.
    c. was one of the Minister's guards.

5. We may infer that

 a. the police noticed the letter, but did not examine it.

 b. the Minister placed the letter where no one could see it.

 c. the Minister was foolish for putting the letter where the Chief could see it.

6. The letter in the letter holder was

 a. tidy and neat.

 b. dirty and torn.

 c. addressed to a member of the government.

7. Which of the following quotations expresses an opinion?

 a. "The next morning I returned for the cigarette case."

 b. "Had I made the wild attempt you suggest, I might never have left him alive."

 c. "I paid special attention to a large desk."

8. Dupin suggested that the Minister "deposited the letter under the nose of the world." What is the meaning of the word *deposited*?

 a. mailed *b.* placed *c.* wrote

9. How do you think the Minister felt when he read the poem?

 a. amused   *c.* furious

 b. pleasantly surprised

10. Which of the following best tells the main idea of this selection?

 a. The Chief is unable to find the letter.

 b. Dupin outwits the Minister.

 c. The Minister knew that his home would be searched.

II. On the Trail

SUPPLYING OMISSIONS

 Often, good detective work means "putting the pieces together" in a case. Sometimes, however, one or more of the pieces may be missing. Then the detective must look closely at the evidence and use his or her reason to supply what is missing, or *omitted*.

The reader as detective also must be able to *supply omissions*. First review the facts found in a story. Then use your reason to supply scenes and events which do not actually appear in the selection. The following questions will help you develop this skill.

11. After he left the Minister's house, Dupin must have

    a. called Chief Gerrard for help.
    b. wondered where the letter was hidden.
    c. made a letter like the one he had seen.

12. Although the scene does not appear in the story, we can be sure that Dupin discussed with another man

    a. how to overpower the Minister's guards.
    b. where and when to fire a gun.
    c. when to attack the Minister.

13. Before Gerrard searched the house, the Minister

    a. hid the letter in the basement.
    b. turned the letter inside out and addressed it again.
    c. put an extra lock on the door.

14. Dupin made two visits to the Minister's house. Between the visits, Dupin

    a. wrote a brief poem.
    b. called the police.
    c. hired a guard to protect him.

15. What did Dupin do with the letter he took from the rack?

    a. He brought it to the police station.
    b. He returned it to an official in the government.
    c. He took it back to his apartment.

III. Finding Word Meanings

Following are five vocabulary words which appear in "The Purloined Letter," Part 2, and five *new* vocabulary words for you to learn. Study the words and their definitions. Then complete the following paragraphs by using each vocabulary word only *once*.

page

intelligence	ability to learn and know	67
probable	likely to happen; likely to be true	68
keen	sharp	69
fascinating	of very great interest	69
exceedingly	very; very greatly	71
trio	group of three	
fictional	made up	
distinction	honor	
critic	a person who judges or gives opinions	
created	brought into being; made	

Edgar Allan Poe was an __16__ important American author. Poe wrote short stories and poems. He was also a noted __17__ of literature. Poe's life and works were unusually interesting and __18__ . Because of this, it is likely, or __19__ , that more books have been written about Poe than about any other American writer.

Poe has earned the honor, or __20__ , of being called the father of the modern American detective story. He __21__ C. Auguste Dupin, the imaginary, or __22__ , detective. Dupin appeared in three of Poe's short stories. "The Purloined Letter" was one of the __23__ . Like Sherlock Holmes, Dupin was a careful, __24__ observer. Like Holmes, Dupin used his __25__ to solve crimes.

IV. Reviewing the Case

Now it's time to review the case. Answer the following questions. Be sure to use complete sentences in your answers.

A. According to Dupin, why did the Minister purposely stay away from his house?

B. Dupin was convinced that to hide the letter, "the Minister had decided on the excellent plan of not hiding it at all." What did Dupin mean by this?

C. When was Dupin sure that he had found the letter for which he was searching?

D. What did Dupin do when the Minister looked out the window?

"You know, I think those two share a secret . . . . It is as though they both sometimes chuckle at us as they go off on their route."

A Secret for Two

by Quentin Reynolds

Montreal is a very large city. But, like all large cities, it has some very small streets. Streets, for instance, like Prince Edward Street, which is only four blocks long and ends in a dead end. No one knew Prince Edward Street as well as Pierre Dupin. Pierre had been delivering milk to the families on the street for thirty years now.

For the past fifteen years, the horse which drew the milk wagon used by Pierre was a large white horse named Joseph. In Montreal, especially in that part which is very French, an animal, like a child, is often given the name of a saint. When the big white horse first came to the Provincale Milk Company, he didn't have a name. They told Pierre that he could use the white horse. Pierre stroked the horse's neck, and he looked into the eyes of the horse.

"This is a kind horse, a gentle and a faithful horse," Pierre said. "I can see a beautiful spirit shining out of the eyes of this horse. I will name him after good St. Joseph, who was also kind and gentle and faithful and a beautiful spirit."

Within a year, Joseph knew the milk route as well as Pierre did. Pierre used to boast that he didn't need reins—he never touched them.

Each morning, Pierre arrived at the stables of the Provincale Milk Company at five o'clock. The wagon would be loaded and Joseph hitched to it. Pierre would call, "*Bon jour, vielle ami* (Hello, old friend)," as he climbed into his seat. Joseph would turn his head, and the other drivers would grin and say that the horse was smiling at Pierre. Then Jacques,

75

the foreman, would say, "All right, Pierre, go on." Pierre would call softly to Joseph, "*Avance, mon ami* (Let's go, my friend)," and this splendid pair would march proudly down the street.

The wagon, without any direction from Pierre, would roll three blocks down St. Catherine Street. Then it would turn right two blocks along Roslyn Avenue. Then left, for that was Prince Edward Street.

The horse would stop at the first house. It would allow Pierre perhaps thirty seconds to get down from his seat and put a bottle of milk at the front door. Then it would go on, skipping two houses, and stopping at the third. So it went, down the length of the street. Then Joseph, still without any direction from Pierre, would turn around and come back along the other side. Yes, Joseph was a smart horse.

At the stable, Pierre would boast of Joseph's skill. "I never touch the reins. He knows just where to stop. Why, a blind man could handle my route with Joseph pulling the wagon." So it went on for years—always the same.

Pierre and Joseph both grew old together, but gradually, not suddenly. Pierre's huge walrus mustache was pure white now and Joseph didn't lift his knees so high or raise his head quite as much. Jacques, the foreman, never noticed that they were both getting old. Then Pierre appeared one day carrying a heavy walking stick.

"Hey, Pierre," Jacques laughed. "Maybe you got the gout, eh?"

"*Mais oui* (Of course), Jacques," Pierre said uneasily. "One grows old. One's legs get tired."

"You should teach the horse to carry the milk to the front door for you," Jacques told him. "He does everything else."

He knew every one of the forty families he served on Prince Edward Street. The cooks knew that Pierre could neither read nor write. So they didn't follow the usual custom of leaving a note in an empty bottle if an additional quart of milk was needed. Instead, when they heard the rumble of his wagon wheels over the cobbled street, they would call out, "Bring an extra quart this morning, Pierre."

Pierre had a wonderful memory. When he arrived at the stable, he'd always remember to tell Jacques, "The Paquins took an extra quart this morning. The Lemoines bought a pint of cream."

Jacques would note these things in a little book he always carried. Most of the drivers had to make out the weekly bills and collect the money. But Jacques liked Pierre and always excused him from this task. All Pierre had to do was arrive at five in the morning, walk to his wagon, which was always in the same spot at the curb, and deliver his milk. He would return later and get down stiffly from his seat. Then, with a cheery "*Au revoir* (Good-bye)" he would limp slowly down the street.

One morning the president of the Provincale Milk Company came to inspect the early morning deliveries. Jacques pointed Pierre out to him and said, "Watch how he talks to that horse. See how the horse listens and how he turns his head toward Pierre. See the look in that horse's eyes. You know, I think those two share a secret. I have often noticed it. It is as though they both sometimes chuckle at us as they go off on their route. Pierre is a good man, Monsieur President, but he is getting old. Would it be too bold for me to suggest that he be retired and be given perhaps a small pension, a modest sum of money?"

"But of course," the president laughed. "I know his record. He has been on this route now for thirty years. Never once has there been a complaint. Tell him it is time he rested. His salary will go on just the same."

But Pierre refused to retire. He was very upset at the thought of not driving Joseph every day. "We are two old men," he said to Jacques. "Let us wear out together. When Joseph is ready to retire—then I, too, will quit."

Jacques, who was a kind man, understood. There was something about Pierre and Joseph which made a man smile tenderly. It was as though each drew some hidden strength from the other. When Pierre was sitting in his seat, and when Joseph was hitched to the wagon, neither seemed old. But when they finished their work, then Pierre would limp down the street slowly. Then he seemed very old indeed. And the horse's head would drop and he would walk very wearily to his stall.

Then one morning Jacques had terrible news for Pierre when he arrived. It was a cold morning and still dark. The air was like ice that morning, and the snow which had fallen during the night glistened like a million diamonds.

Jacques said, "Pierre, your horse, Joseph, did not wake this morning. He was very old, Pierre. He was twenty-five, and that is like seventy-five for a man."

"Yes," Pierre said slowly. "Yes. I am seventy-five. And I cannot see Joseph again."

"Of course you can," Jacques soothed. "He is over in his stall, looking very peaceful. Go over and see him."

Pierre took one step forward then turned. "No . . . no . . . you don't understand, Jacques."

Jacques clapped him on the shoulder. "We'll find another horse just as good as Joseph. Why, in a month you'll teach him to know your route as well as Joseph did. We'll . . . ."

The look in Pierre's eyes stopped him. For years Pierre had worn a heavy cap. The peak of it came low over his eyes. Now Jacques looked into Pierre's eyes and he saw something which startled him. He saw a dead, lifeless look in them. The eyes were mirroring the grief that was in Pierre's heart and his soul. It was as though his heart and soul had died.

"Take today off, Pierre," Jacques said. But already Pierre was hobbling off down the street. Had you been near, you would have seen tears streaming down his cheeks. You would have heard soft sobs. Pierre walked to the corner and stepped into the street. There was a warning yell from the driver of a huge truck that was coming fast. There was the scream of brakes. But Pierre, it seems, heard neither.

Five minutes later an ambulance driver said, "He's dead. Was killed instantly."

Jacques and several of the milk-wagon drivers had arrived. They looked down at the still figure.

"I couldn't help it," the driver of the truck protested. "He walked right into my truck. He never saw it, I guess. Why, he walked into it as though he were blind."

Now it's time for YOU to be The Reader as Detective.

What do you think the ambulance driver said? The hints in the story should help you answer correctly. Read on and see if you are right.

The ambulance driver bent down. "Blind? Of course the man was blind. This man has been blind for five years." He turned to Jacques. "You say he worked for you? Didn't you know he was blind?"

"No . . . no . . . ," Jacques said softly. "None of us knew. Only one knew—a friend of his named Joseph. It was a secret, I think, just between those two."

I. The Reader as Detective

Read each of the following questions. Then write the letter of the correct answer to each question. Remember, the symbol next to each question identifies the *kind* of reading skill that particular question helps you to develop.

 1. Prince Edward Street is very

   a. long.   *b.* small.   *c.* wide.

 2. Pierre had been working for the Provincale Milk Company for

   a. 15 years.   *b.* 25 years.   *c.* 30 years.

 3. We may infer that

   a. Pierre hated his work.
   b. Pierre and Joseph loved each other dearly.
   c. Pierre thought he would find another horse just as good as Joseph.

 4. The president of the milk company came "to inspect the early morning deliveries." Which word or expression means the same as *inspect*?

   a. look over carefully
   b. drive
   c. worry about

 5. Which of the following is true of Pierre?

   a. He was in perfect health.
   b. He had a wonderful memory.
   c. He was very wealthy.

 6. Which happened last?

   a. Jacques told Pierre that Joseph had died.
   b. A truck headed toward Pierre.
   c. The ambulance driver reported that Pierre was blind.

 7. Which of the following is an opinion?

   a. Prince Edward Street is in Montreal.
   b. A horse is a better pet than a dog.
   c. Pierre didn't make out the weekly bills.

8. Jacques suggested that Pierre be offered "a modest sum of money." Which of the following best defines the word *modest*?

    a. not very great   *c.* tiny
    b. quite large

9. Pierre probably didn't hear the truck because

    a. he was deaf.
    b. he was thinking about Joseph.
    c. he was worried about losing his job.

10. This story is mainly about

    a. a day in the life of Pierre.
    b. how the president of a milk company offered Pierre a pension.
    c. two old friends and the secret they shared.

II. On the Trail

HINTS AND SUGGESTIONS

At the conclusion of "A Secret for Two," we are told that Pierre "has been blind for five years." How good a reading detective were you? Did the ending surprise you—or did you detect the *hints* and *suggestions* about Pierre's condition?

The following questions will provide practice and review in recognizing hints.

11. Below are three statements made by Pierre. Which one suggests how the story will end?

    a. "Yes, I am seventy-five."
    b. "The Paquins took an extra quart this morning."
    c. "Why, a blind man could handle my route with Joseph pulling the wagon."

12. Pierre didn't have to read the usual notes left in empty bottles because

    a. the orders were always the same.
    b. Jacques excused Pierre from this task.
    c. the cooks called out the orders to Pierre.

13. For years, Pierre wore a cap whose peak ''came low over his eyes.'' Probably, Pierre did this because

    a. he wanted to keep the sun out of his eyes.
    b. he didn't want anyone to see his eyes.
    c. he liked the way he looked wearing a cap.

14. What did Pierre say when he learned that Joseph had died?

    a. ''He (Joseph) was as old as a man of seventy-five.''
    b. ''I cannot see Joseph again.''
    c. ''No one can learn my route as well as Joseph did.''

15. What did Jacques see when he looked into Pierre's eyes?

    a. a dead, lifeless look
    b. a hopeful look
    c. a look of joy

Note that the correct answer to each question provides a hint or suggestion to the fact that Pierre was blind.

III. Finding Word Meanings

Listed below are five vocabulary words which appear in ''A Secret for Two'' and five *new* vocabulary words for you to learn. Study the words and their definitions. Then complete the following paragraphs by using each vocabulary word only *once*.

		page
splendid	very fine; excellent	76
additional	extra; added; more	77
pension	regular payment of money for long service to someone who has reached a certain age	78
complaint	a finding of fault; finding fault	78
retire	rest; give up a job because of age	78
rejected	refused	
devoted	faithful; loyal	
appreciated	thought highly of; valued	
demonstrated	showed	
preferred	liked better; chose	

"A Secret for Two" is an excellent, a truly __16__ story. In it, we meet Pierre Dupin and his very faithful, or __17__, horse, Joseph. Pierre and Joseph were a wonderful team. Each day, without __18__, Joseph helped Pierre with his chores. Pierre, in turn, trusted his friend; he valued and __19__ Joseph more and more because he knew he couldn't get along without him. As Pierre grew older, Joseph gladly took on __20__ responsibilities.

Through their daily actions, Pierre and Joseph __21__ great love for each other. Because of Joseph, Pierre was unwilling to __22__, even though they both were getting old. Pierre's company offered him a __23__, but he __24__ it. The reason he refused it was that Pierre __25__ to stay on the job as long as Joseph could still work.

IV. Reviewing the Case

Now it's time to review the case. Using complete sentences, briefly answer the following.

1. Pierre once said, "When Joseph is ready to retire—then I, too, will quit."
   A. Why do you think Pierre felt this way?
   B. Show how Pierre did "quit" after Joseph died.

2. Make a list of the clues which suggest that Pierre was blind. Refer to your list to write a paragraph with the following opening sentence:

   Before the ambulance driver revealed that Pierre was blind, there were many hints that this was so.

Note: If you have sufficient clues, add a second paragraph.

Sarah Tops

by Isaac Asimov

I came out of the Museum of Natural History and was crossing the street on my way to the subway. That's when I saw the crowd about halfway down the block. I saw the police cars, too. I could hear the whine of an ambulance.

For a minute I hesitated. But then I walked on. Folks who are curious just get in the way of people trying to save lives. Dad, who's a detective on the force, complains about that all the time.

I just kept my mind on the term paper I was going to have to write on air pollution for my 8th-grade class. I thought about the notes I had taken on the subject while I was at the museum.

Of course, I knew I would read about what had happened in the museum in tomorrow's newspaper. Besides, I would ask Dad about it after dinner. He sometimes talked about cases without telling too much of the real private details.

After Dad told us, Mom looked kind of worried. She said, "The man was killed in the museum. You were in the museum, Larry."

I said, "I was working on my term paper. I got there early in the morning."

Mom looked very worried. "There might have been shooting in the museum."

"Well, there wasn't," said Dad, softly. "This man tried to hide himself there and he didn't succeed."

"I would have," I said. "I know the museum, every inch."

Dad doesn't like me bragging. So he frowned a little and

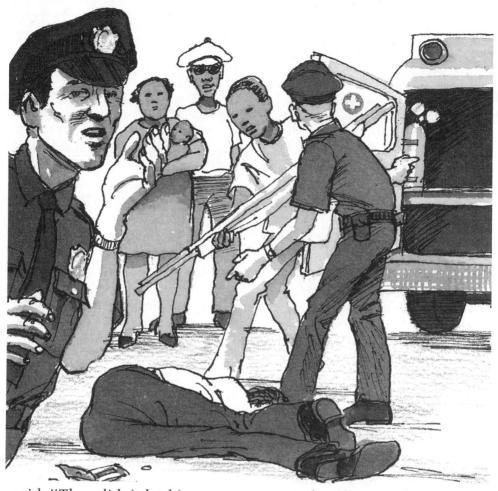

said, "They didn't let him get away entirely. They caught up with him outside. They knifed him and got away. We'll catch them, though. We know who they are."

He nodded his head. "They're what's left of that gang that broke into that jewelry store two weeks ago. We managed to get the jewels back. But we didn't grab all the men. We didn't get all the jewels back either. One diamond was left. A big one—worth $30,000."

"Maybe that's what the killers were after," I said.

"Very likely. The dead man was probably trying to cross up the other two. He was probably trying to get away with that one stone for himself. They turned out his pockets, nearly ripped off his clothes, after they knifed him."

"Did they get the diamond?" I asked.

"How can we tell? The woman who reported the killing found him when he was just barely alive. She said he said three words to her, very slowly, 'Try—Sarah—Tops.' Then he died."

"Who is Sarah Tops?" asked Mom.

Dad shrugged. "I don't know. I don't even know if that's really what he said. The woman was pretty hysterical. If she's right and that's what he said, then maybe the killers didn't get the diamond. Maybe the dead man left it with Sarah Tops, whoever she is."

"Is there a Sarah Tops in the phone book, Dad?" I asked.

Dad said, "Did you think we didn't look? No Sarah Tops, either with one **P** or two **P**'s. Nothing in the city phone book. Nothing in our files. Nothing in the FBI files."

Mom said, "Maybe it's not a person. Maybe it's a company. Sarah Tops cakes or something."

"Could be," said Dad. "There's no Sarah Tops company. But there are other kinds of Tops companies. They'll be checked for anyone working there named Sarah."

Suddenly I got an idea and bubbled over. "Listen, Dad, maybe it isn't a company either. Maybe it's a *thing*. Maybe the woman didn't hear 'Sarah Tops' but heard 'Sarah's top.' You know, a *top* that you *spin*. If the dead guy has a daughter named Sarah, maybe he cut a bit out of her top and stashed the diamond inside. Maybe—"

Dad grinned. "Very good, Larry," he said. "But he doesn't have a daughter named Sarah. Or any relative by that name as far as we know. We've searched where he lived. There's nothing reported there that can be called a top."

I felt sort of let down and disappointed. "Well," I said, "I suppose that's not such a good idea anyway. Because why should he say we ought to *try* it? He either hid it in Sarah's top or he didn't. He would know which. Why should he say we should *try* it?"

And then it hit me. What if—

I said, "Dad, can you get into the museum this late?"

"On police business? Sure."

"Dad," I said, kind of breathless, "I think we better go look. *Now*. Before the people start coming in again."

"Why?"

"I've got a silly idea. I— I—"

Dad didn't push me. He likes me to have my own ideas. He thinks maybe I'll be a detective too, some day. He said, "All right. Let's follow up your lead."

We got there just when the last purple bit of twilight was turning to black. We were let in by a guard.

I'd never been in the museum when it was dark. It looked like a huge underground cave. The guard's flashlight made things even more mysterious.

We took the elevator up to the fourth floor. I could see the big shapes in the bit of light that shone this way and that as the guard moved his flashlight. "Do you want me to put on the light in this room?" he asked.

"Yes, please," I said.

There they all were. Some were in glass cases. But the big ones were in the middle of the large room. Bones and teeth and spines of giants that ruled the earth millions of years ago. I said, "I want to look close at that one. Is it all right if I climb over the railing?"

"Go ahead," said the guard. He helped me.

I leaned against the platform. I was looking at the gray plaster material that the dinosaur was standing on.

Suddenly I spotted something. "What's this?" I said. It didn't look much different in color from the plaster.

"Chewing gum," said the guard, frowning. "Those darn kids—"

I said, "The guy was trying to get away. He saw his chance to throw this—to hide it from the gang—"

Dad took the gum from me. He squeezed the gum. Then he pulled it apart. Inside, something caught the light and flashed. Dad put the diamond in an envelope. Then he said to me, "How did you know?"

Now it's time for YOU to be The Reader as Detective.

How did Larry know where to look for the diamond? Think back to what the dying man said. Then read on.

I said, "Just look at that."

It was an amazing dinosaur. It had a large skull with long bones stretching back over the neck. It had two horns over the eyes, and a third one, just a bump, on the nose. The name-plate said: Triceratops.

I. The Reader as Detective

Read each of the following questions. Then write the letter of the correct answer to each question. Remember, the symbol next to each question identifies the *kind* of reading skill that particular question helps you to develop.

 1. The man was killed

   a. in a jewelry store.
   b. on his way to the subway.
   c. in the Museum of Natural History.

 2. Dad said that the diamond was worth

   a. $300.
   b. $3,000.
   c. $30,000.

 3. What happened after the guard turned on the light in the museum?

   a. Larry began to look through the notes he had taken.
   b. Larry climbed over the railing.
   c. They all took the elevator to the fourth floor.

 4. Larry's father was "a detective on the force." As used in this sentence, what is the meaning of the word *force*?

   a. power
   b. army or navy
   c. group of people who work together

 5. Why do you think Larry wanted to go to the museum right away?

   a. He wanted to finish his term paper.
   b. He was afraid that someone else might find the diamond first.
   c. He thought that the murderer might be hiding there.

6. Larry's Dad thought that Larry might become a

   a. scientist.   *c.* teacher.

   b. detective.

7. Which of the following is *not* an opinion?

   a. The Museum of Natural History is the best museum in the world.

   b. Isaac Asimov is the author of "Sarah Tops."

   c. Being a detective is the most dangerous job anyone can have.

8. Larry heard "the whine of an ambulance." Which of the following best defines the word *whine*?

   a. screaming, complaining sound   *c.* ringing bells

   b. squeaking brakes

9. Larry said that he knew

   a. every inch of the museum.

   b. how to get into the museum.

   c. the name of the murderer.

10. Suppose this story appeared as a news article in a newspaper. Which of the following would make the best headline?

   a. Detective's Son Solves Museum Murder Case

   b. Man Tries to Hide in Museum—Doesn't Succeed

   c. Larry and His Father Discuss Man Killed in Museum

II. On the Trail

DRAWING CONCLUSIONS

As you know, a good reader *draws conclusions.* These conclusions are based on facts and story clues found in the selection. As the reader as detective, you must learn to draw conclusions. The following questions will help you practice this skill.

11. We may conclude that the dying man

   a. gave the diamond to Sarah Tops.

   b. nearly got away from his killers.

   c. hid the diamond in the chewing gum.

12. As you know, the prefix *tri* means *three*. Therefore, the dinosaur was probably called *triceratops* because it

     a. was more than twice as tall as any dinosaur.
     b. had an enormous skull.
     c. had three horns.

13. It was hard to find the gum because

     a. the room was so dark.
     b. it was almost the same color as the plaster.
     c. it wasn't hidden in the museum.

14. Larry's actions suggest that he is

     a. thoughtful and smart.
     b. a poor student.
     c. smart but lazy.

15. It is correct to conclude that

     a. some kids stuck the gum on the plaster.
     b. the guard knew where the diamond was hidden.
     c. the dying man was trying to say "Triceratops."

III. Finding Word Meanings

Listed below are five vocabulary words which appear in "Sarah Tops" and five *new* vocabulary words for you to learn. Study the words and their definitions. Then complete the following paragraphs by using each vocabulary word only *once*.

		page
pollution	the dirtying of conditions that affect the growth of life	84
bragging	praising or boasting about oneself	84
entirely	completely	85
hysterical	highly excited; out of self-control	86
stashed	hid	86
embarrassed	made uneasy and ashamed	
considerable	not a little; much	
impressed	had a strong effect on; moved	
despair	loss of hope	
survey	to look over	

Larry could not find the report he had written on air __16__ . After searching for it for half an hour, he was so excited that he was nearly __17__ . He had spent a __18__ amount of time working on the paper, and now it was missing. To make matters worse, he had been very pleased and __19__ by how good the report was. He had even been __20__ to his friends about how good it was. If he could not find it, he was going to be ashamed, or __21__ , in class.

Larry began to __22__ the room again. He had already looked through it __23__ . Suddenly, Larry remembered something. For safe-keeping, he had __24__ the report in the bottom drawer of his desk. Larry's deep __25__ turned to relief as he saw it lying safely there.

IV. Reviewing the Case

Now it's time to review the case. Larry's Dad must have been proud of Larry for having solved the case. What do you think he might have told the other detectives at the station house later? In about 100 words, write what you think Larry's father might have said. Be sure to put quotation marks around his words.

Afterwards, you may have an opportunity to share your writing with the class, and to select the compositions you liked best.

One Throw

by W. C. Heinz

I checked into a hotel called the Olympia, which is right on the main street and the only hotel in the town. After lunch I was hanging around the lobby, and I got to talking to the guy at the desk. I asked him if this wasn't the town where that kid named Maneri played ball.

"That's right," the guy said. "He's a pretty good ballplayer."

"He should be," I said. "I read that he was the new Phil Rizzuto."*

"That's what they said," the guy said.

"What's the matter with him?" I said. "I mean—if he's such a good ballplayer, what's he doing in this league?"

"I don't know," the guy said. "I guess the Yankees know what they're doing."

"He lives here in this hotel?"

"That's right," the guy said. "Most of the older ballplayers stay in rooming houses, but Pete and a couple other kids live here."

He was leaning on the desk, talking to me and looking across the little lobby. He nodded his head. "Here he comes now."

The kid had come through the door from the street. I could see why, when he showed up with the Yankees in spring training, he made them all think of Rizzuto. He isn't any bigger than Rizzuto, and he looks just like him.

---

*Phil Rizzuto: a great baseball player for the New York Yankees. Rizzuto, who was five feet six inches tall, played shortstop.

"Hello, Nick," he said to the guy at the desk.

"Hello, Pete," the guy at the desk said. "How goes it to-day?"

"All right," the kid said, but you could see that he was exaggerating.

"I'm sorry, Pete," the guy at the desk said, "but no mail today."

"That's all right, Nick," the kid said. "I'm used to it."

"Excuse me," I said, "but you're Pete Maneri?"

"That's right," the kid said, turning and looking at me.

"Excuse me," the guy at the desk said, introducing us. "Pete, this is Mr. Franklin."

"Harry Franklin," I said.

"I'm glad to know you," the kid said, shaking my hand.

"I recognize you from your pictures," I said.

"Pete's a good ballplayer," the guy at the desk said.

"Not very," the kid said.

"Don't take his word for it, Mr. Franklin," the guy said.

"I'm a great ball fan," I said to the kid. "Do you people play tonight?"

"We play two games," the kid said.

"That first game's at six o'clock," the guy at the desk said. "They play pretty good ball."

"I'll be there," I said. "I used to play a little ball myself."

"You did?" the kid said.

"With Columbus," I said. "That was twenty years ago."

"Is that right?" the kid said . . .

That's the way I got to talking with the kid. They had one of those pine-paneled grill rooms in the basement of the hotel, and we went down there. I had a cup of coffee and the kid had a Coke, and I told him a few stories and he turned out to be a real good listener.

"But what do you do now, Mr. Franklin?" he said after a while.

"I sell hardware," I said. "I can think of some things I'd like better, but I was going to ask you how you like playing in this league."

"Well," the kid said, "I guess I've got no kick coming."

"Oh, I don't know," I said. "I understand you're too good for this league. What are they trying to do to you?"

"I don't know," the kid said. "I can't understand it."

"What's the trouble?"

"Well," the kid said, "there's nothing wrong with my play-ing. I'm hitting .365 right now. I lead the league in stolen bases. There's nobody can field with me, but who cares?"

"Who manages this ball club?"

"Al Dall," the kid said. "You remember, he played in the outfield for the Yankees for about four years."

"I remember."

"Maybe he's all right," the kid said, "but I don't get along with him. He's on my neck all the time."

"Well," I said, "that's the way they are in the minors sometimes. You have to remember the guy is looking out for himself and his ball club first."

"I know that," the kid said. "If I get the big hit or make the play, he never says anything. The other night I tried to take second on a loose ball and I got caught in the rundown. He bawled me out in front of everybody. There's nothing I can do."

"Oh, I don't know," I said. "This is probably a guy who

knows he's got a good thing in you, and he's trying to keep you around. You people lead the league, and that makes him look good. He doesn't want to lose you to Kansas City or the Yankees."

"That's what I mean," the kid said. "When the Yankees sent me down here they said, 'Don't worry. We'll keep an eye on you.' So Dall never sends back a good report on me. Nobody ever comes down to look me over. What chance is there for a guy like Eddie Brown to see me in this town?"

"You have to remember that Eddie Brown's the big shot," I said, "the great Yankee scout."

"Sure," the kid said, "and I'll never see him in this place. I have an idea that if they ever ask Dall about me, he keeps knocking me down."

"Why don't you go after Dall?" I said. "I had trouble like that once myself, but I figured out a way to get attention."

"You did?" the kid said.

"I threw a couple of balls over the first baseman's head," I said. "I threw a couple of games away, and that really made the manager sore. So what does he do? He blows the whistle on me, and what happens? That gets the top brass curious, and they send down to see what's wrong."

"Is that so?" the kid said. "What happened?"

"Two weeks later," I said, "I was up with Columbus."

"Is that right?" the kid said.

"Sure," I said, egging him on. "What have you got to lose?"

"Nothing," the kid said. "I haven't got anything to lose."

"I'd try it," I said.

"I might," the kid said. "I might try it tonight if the spot comes up."

I could see from the way he said it that he was madder than he'd said. Maybe you think this is mean to steam a kid up like this, but I do some strange things.

"Take over," I said. "Don't let this guy ruin your career."

"I'll try it," the kid said. "Are you coming out to the park tonight?"

"I wouldn't miss it," I said. "This will be better than making out route sheets and sales orders."

It's not much of a ball park in this town—old wooden bleachers and an old wooden fence and about four hundred people in the stands. The first game wasn't much of a game either, with the home club winning something like 8 to 1.

The kid didn't have any hard chances, but I could see he was a ballplayer, with a double and a couple of walks and a lot of speed.

The second game was different, though. The other club got a couple of runs and then the home club picked up three runs in one inning. In the top of the ninth the home club had a 3–2 lead and two outs when the pitching began to fall apart and the other club loaded the bases.

I was trying to wish the ball down to the kid, just to see what he'd do with it, when the batter drove one on one bounce to the kid's right.

The kid was off for it when the ball started. He made a backhand stab and grabbed it. He was deep now, and he turned in the air and fired. If it goes over the first baseman's head it's two runs in and a panic—but it's the prettiest throw you'd want to see. It's right on a line, and the runner is out by a step, and it's the ball game.

I walked back to the hotel, thinking about the kid. I sat around the lobby until I saw him come in, and then I walked toward the elevator as if I were going to my room, but so I'd meet him. I could see he didn't want to talk.

"How about a Coke?" I said.

"No," he said. "Thanks, but I'm going to bed."

"Look," I said. "Forget it. You did the right thing. Have a Coke."

We were sitting in the grill room again. The kid wasn't saying anything.

"Why didn't you throw that ball away?" I said.

"I don't know," the kid said. "I had the idea in my mind before he hit it, but I couldn't."

"Why?"

"I don't know why."

"I know why," I said.

The kid didn't say anything. He just sat there, looking down.

"Do you know why you couldn't throw that ball away?" I said.

"No," the kid said.

"You couldn't throw that ball away," I said, "because you're going to be a major-league ballplayer someday."

The kid just looked at me. He had that same sore expression.

"Do you know why you're going to be a major-league ballplayer?" I said.

> Now it's time for YOU to be The Reader as Detective.
>
> How did Harry Franklin know that Maneri would be a major-league ballplayer? You should be able to guess. Read on to see if you are right.

The kid was just looking down again, shaking his head. I never got more of a kick out of anything in my life.

"You're going to be a major-league ballplayer," I said, "because you couldn't throw that ball away, and because I'm not Harry Franklin."

"What do you mean?" the kid said.

"I mean," I explained to him, "that I tried to needle you into throwing that ball away because I'm Eddie Brown."

I. The Reader as Detective

Read each of the following questions. Then write the letter of the correct answer to each question. Remember, the symbol next to each question identifies the *kind* of reading skill that particular question helps you to develop.

1. Pete Maneri looked like
   a. Phil Rizzuto.   *c.* Eddie Brown.
   b. Harry Franklin.

2. Mr. Franklin said that he
   a. worked in a hotel.   *c.* sold hardware.
   b. managed the Yankees.

3. Harry Franklin tried to "needle" Pete into throwing the ball away. Which word or expression best defines the word *needle* as used in this sentence?

  a. threaten
  b. urge on
  c. an instrument used in sewing

4. According to Maneri, Al Dall

  a. sent back good reports on him.
  b. bawled him out in front of everybody.
  c. was very friendly to him.

5. Probably, Franklin suggested that Maneri throw the ball away because he

  a. wanted the home team to lose the game.
  b. wanted Maneri to make an error.
  c. wanted to see if Maneri placed winning over personal gain.

6. Which of the following is an opinion?

  a. Maneri led the league in stolen bases.
  b. Maneri was batting .365 in the minor leagues.
  c. Maneri is sure to lead the major leagues in batting one day.

7. Had the ball gone over the first baseman's head, it would have been "two runs in and a panic." Which of the following best defines the word *panic*?

  a. tie score
  b. wild result
  c. difficult question

8. Which of the following is true of Maneri?

  a. He was a poor fielder.
  b. He lived in a rooming house.
  c. He had lots of speed.

9. Which happened last?

  a. The man at the desk introduced Pete to Mr. Franklin.
  b. Harry Franklin told Pete his real name.
  c. Maneri said he might throw a ball away.

10. This story is mainly about

    a. how Pete Maneri made a bad throw and lost the game for his team.

    b. how a minor-league ball player proves himself to a big-league scout.

    c. how Eddie Brown checked into the Olympia Hotel on the main street in town.

II. On the Trail

STORY CLUES

Did you realize that Harry Franklin was Eddie Brown? If so, when did you first suspect this? Try the following questions. Each correct answer provides a story *clue* to the fact that Harry Franklin was Eddie Brown.

11. Which of the following suggests that Harry Franklin was really a scout?

    a. He used to play baseball with Columbus.

    b. He enjoyed talking to Maneri.

    c. He heard that Maneri was angry at Al Dall.

12. Which of the following is a clue that Franklin wasn't telling the truth about who he was?

    a. He said he made out route sheets and sales orders.

    b. He said he sometimes did strange things.

    c. He could see that Maneri was madder than he'd said.

13. During the game, Maneri "didn't have any hard chances." However, Franklin

    a. didn't mind coming back to see him another day.

    b. could see that he was a good ballplayer.

    c. thought the home team was outstanding.

14. Franklin had heard that Maneri was

    a. too good for his league.

    b. much taller than Rizzuto.

    c. not a very good fielder.

15. Franklin told Maneri that he

 a. should try his best every game.
 b. should listen to his manager.
 c. was going to be a major-league ballplayer.

 Notice how the correct answer to each question is a clue to the fact that Harry Franklin was a scout.

III. Finding Word Meanings

 Listed below are five vocabulary words which appear in "One Throw" and five *new* vocabulary words for you to learn. Study the words and their definitions. Then complete the following paragraphs by using each vocabulary word only *once*.

		page
lobby	entrance hall	92
exaggerating	going beyond the truth	93
sore	angry; painful	95
career	life's work; way of living	95
bleachers	benches or stands for the fans at sporting events	95
abundant	many; more than enough	
discouraging	causing to lose hope	
luxurious	comfortable and pleasant	
achievement	something carried out successfully	
lounging	passing time lazily	

 It would not be overstating, or __16__ , to say that making it to the major leagues is an __17__ truly worthy of note. Most would-be big leaguers must spend years in the minors. There they have a great many, or __18__, opportunities to sharpen their skills. But life in the minors is difficult and __19__ . There are long, tiring bus rides, and games played before __20__ which may contain only a hundred or so fans.

 Living conditions in the minors are not very comfortable and are certainly not __21__ . Players spend lazy hours __22__ in their rooms or in the front __23__ of the hotel. And, of course, there are the __24__ and aching bones which come with playing almost every day. Still, players who hope for a ___25___ in the major leagues are willing to put up with these conditions.

IV. Reviewing the Case

Now it's time to review the case. Life in the minor leagues is usually very lonely. Therefore, players call or write home frequently to receive and share news.

Suppose Pete Maneri wrote a letter home describing what occurred with Mr. Franklin. What do you think he would say? Write Pete's letter. Address it to "Dear Folks."

First make a rough draft of your letter. Proofread it carefully, making corrections. Then write the final draft of your letter.

"At the doorway, De Ville turned his head. He shot a swift look back at his enemy. The look troubled me at the time. For not only did I see hatred in it, I saw triumph as well."

The Leopard Man's Story

by Jack London

He had a dreamy, faraway look in his eyes, and his voice was soft and gentle. He was thin and pale, and he seemed very sad. He was the Leopard Man, though he did not look it.

He earned his living working at a circus. Every day he climbed into a cage filled with leopards. He thrilled vast audiences with his skill and nerve. For this he was well paid.

For an hour I had been trying to get a story out of him. But he could think of nothing to tell me. He did not consider his work dangerous or daring. He did not think it thrilling. To him it was a job, one that sometimes became boring.

"How about lions?" I asked.

"Oh yes," he said. "I have often fought with them. But it is nothing. All one must do is stay alert. Anyone can whip a lion with an ordinary stick. I fought one for half an hour once. Just hit him on the nose every time he rushed. That was all."

He showed me his scars. There were many of them. I saw a recent one. A tiger had clawed his shoulder and cut him to the bone. His right arm, from his elbow down, was filled with old wounds. "It is nothing," he said. "Only they sometimes bother me when the rainy weather comes."

Suddenly his face brightened with a recollection. For he was really as eager to give me a story as I was to get one.

"Let me tell you about a fellow I knew. He was a little, thin, sword-swallowing knife-thrower. He called himself De Ville. Now this De Ville had a quick temper, as quick as his hand; and his hand was as quick as the paw of a tiger.

"One day the ringmaster called De Ville a name. De Ville shoved him against the wooden board that he used in his knife-throwing act. He did it so quickly, the ringmaster didn't have time to think. There, in front of the audience, De Ville filled the air with knives. He sunk them into the wood all around the ringmaster. They were so close that they passed through his clothes and just touched his skin. The clowns had to pull out the knives to get him loose. So the word went around the circus to watch out for De Ville.

"But there was one man, Wallace, who was afraid of nothing—not even De Ville. Wallace was the lion tamer. He used to put his head into the mouth of a lion. Any lion would do. But he preferred Augustus, a big, good-natured beast.

"As I was saying, Wallace—'King' Wallace we called him—was afraid of nothing. He really was a king, make no mistake about it. I saw him, on a wager, go into the cage of a lion that had turned nasty. Without a stick Wallace beat that lion. Just did it with his fist."

The Leopard Man paused. He looked thoughtfully at a sick lion in a nearby cage. Then he continued.

"One day 'King' Wallace and De Ville got into a fight. Wallace picked up De Ville and dropped him into a bucket of water. Then laughing at him, Wallace walked away.

"De Ville was soaked. He must have been furious. But he stayed cool as a cucumber and made no threat at all. However, I saw a glitter in his eyes which I had often seen in the eyes of wild beasts. I warned Wallace, but he only laughed at me.

"Several months passed by. Nothing had happened and I was beginning to think it was a scare over nothing. By that time we had arrived out West in San Francisco. The afternoon show was going on, and the big tent was filled. I was looking for Red Denny, who had walked off with my pocket-knife.

"As I walked past one of the dressing tents, I glanced through a hole in the canvas to see if I could find him. Red

Denny wasn't there. But right in front of me was 'King' Wallace. He was waiting to go on with his lions.

"Wallace was watching with amusement a quarrel between two acrobats. Everyone was looking at them closely—all except De Ville. He was staring with undisguised hatred at Wallace. They were all too busy to notice what happened next. But I saw it through the hole in the canvas.

"De Ville carefully took his handkerchief from his pocket. He made believe he was wiping the sweat from his face with it, for it was a very hot day. Then he began to walk toward the exit of the tent. As he brushed by behind Wallace's back, he shook out the handkerchief. At the doorway, De Ville

turned his head. He shot a swift look back at his enemy. The look troubled me at the time. For not only did I see hatred in it, I saw triumph as well.

"I must watch De Ville," I thought to myself. "And I breathed easier when I saw him leave the circus grounds.

"A few minutes later, I found Red Denny in the big tent. 'King' Wallace's act had just begun. He was in particularly good form and was keeping the audience spellbound. He kept all the lions stirred up, snarling and growling around him. All of them, that is, except old Augustus. He was just too fat and too lazy to get excited about anything.

"Finally Wallace cracked his whip to get the old lion into position. Augustus blinked good-naturedly and opened his mouth. In went Wallace's head. Then the jaws came together, *crunch*, just like that."

The Leopard Man smiled in a sorrowful way, and the far-away look came into his eyes.

"And that was the end of 'King' Wallace," he went on in a sad, low voice. "After the excitement cooled down I watched my chance. I bent over and smelled Wallace's head. Then I sneezed."

"It . . . it was . . .?" I asked, eager to know.

> Now it's time for YOU to be The Reader as Detective.
>
> What do you think the Leopard Man answered?
> Think back to the story before you answer. Then read on to see if you are right.

"Pepper—that De Ville dropped on his hair in the dressing tent. Old Augustus never meant to do it. He just sneezed."

I. The Reader as Detective

Read each of the following questions. Then write the letter of the correct answer to each question. Remember, the symbol next to each question identifies the *kind* of reading skill that particular question helps you to develop.

1. The Leopard Man thought that his job was

   a. very dangerous.

   b. thrilling.

   c. sometimes boring.

2. "King" Wallace was afraid of

   a. Augustus.   *b.* De Ville.   *c.* nobody.

3. Which happened first?

   a. The ringmaster called De Ville a name.

   b. Everyone watched a quarrel between two acrobats.

   c. Wallace dropped De Ville into a bucket of water.

4. The Leopard Man "glanced through a hole in the canvas." As used in this sentence, what is the meaning of the word *glanced?*

   a. hit sharply   *c.* flashed with light

   b. looked quickly

5. What did De Ville do to the ringmaster?

   a. He shoved him against a wooden board.

   b. He threw knives close to him.

   c. both of the above.

6. We may infer that De Ville

   a. sprinkled some pepper onto his handkerchief.

   b. was not really angry at Wallace.

   c. had not worked at the circus very long.

7. Which of the following is a fact?

   a. It is more fun to go to the circus than to go to a ball game.

   b. The Leopard Man was usually very cheerful.

   c. The Leopard Man was pale and thin.

8. On a wager, "King" Wallace went into the cage of a lion that had turned nasty. Which of the following best defines the word *wager?*

   a. wish   *b.* bet   *c.* small wagon

9. Which of the following is probably true?

  a. De Ville was sorry for what he had done to Wallace.
  b. Old Augustus later missed Wallace.
  c. The circus closed forever because of Wallace's death.

 10. Which sentence best gives the main idea of the story?

  a. A circus performer gets even with his enemy.
  b. Working in a circus can be very dangerous.
  c. Most old lions are fat and lazy.

II. On the Trail

STORY CLUES

As you know, story clues are hints or signposts that point the way to how the story will end. How good a reading detective were you? Did you spot the story clues in "The Leopard Man's Story"?

Think about the story. Then answer the following questions. Each is based on a story clue found in the selection.

11. Each of the following sentences appears in "The Leopard Man's Story." Which one suggests how De Ville will get revenge on Wallace?

  a. But De Ville stayed as cool as a cucumber and made no threat at all.
  b. The afternoon show was going on, and the big tent was filled.
  c. De Ville had a quick temper, as quick as his hand; and his hand was as quick as the paw of a tiger.

12. De Ville put pepper on Wallace's head when he

  a. "brushed by behind Wallace's back" and "shook out the handkerchief."
  b. "shoved him against the wooden board."
  c. "filled the air with knives."

13. The reader should be suspicious about the handkerchief because De Ville

  a. seldom had a handkerchief with him.
  b. hid the handkerchief in his pocket.
  c. made believe he was wiping the sweat from his brow with it.

14. The Leopard Man was afraid of what De Ville might do because De Ville

    a. warned Wallace to stay away from him.
    b. had in his eyes the glitter of a wild beast.
    c. was very friendly with the acrobats.

15. The reader should realize that De Ville had succeeded in his plan when he

    a. shot a look of triumph at his enemy.
    b. saw Wallace watching a quarrel.
    c. stared at Wallace with hatred.

Review your answers to the questions above. Notice how they provide clues to how the story will end.

III. Finding Word Meanings

The ten words listed below appear in "The Leopard Man's Story." Study the words and their definitions. If you like, look back to the story to see how the words are used.

Then complete the following paragraphs by using each vocabulary word only *once*. The definitions, and the context clues in the passage, will help you select the correct word.

		page
thrilled	excited	102
vast	very great	102
scars	marks left by a wound	102
recollection	memory	102
nasty	mean or cruel	103
threat	sign or cause of harm	103
amusement	pleasure	104
undisguised	not hidden; open	104
triumph	success; victory	105
spellbound	too interested to move	105

The stories and novels of Jack London have excited and __16__ a __17__ number of readers. Audiences all over the world have been held __18__ by his tales. Few authors have provided so many people with such pleasure, or __19__ .

Many of London's works are obviously based on actual, and
__20__ , events that he experienced during his lifetime. For the plots
of his novels, for example, London often drew upon his memory, or
__21__ , of his days as a sailor.

You might think that London's life was filled only with __22__ and
success. However, this was not so. When he was still a young man,
London was struck by a __23__ illness. For years it was a __24__ to his
life. London never recovered from the __25__ it left on him. He died
when he was only 40 years old.

IV. Reviewing the Case

Now it's time to review the case. Pretend that *you* are De Ville
and that you have decided to confess your crime to the police. In
two or three paragraphs, write your confession . Explain the reasons
for your crime, and how you planned it and carried it out.

Later, volunteers may have an opportunity to read their confession to the police (the class).

"I'm going to give you a magic word. All you have to do is repeat this magic charm once and no dragon can possibly harm a hair of your head."

The Fifty-First Dragon

by Heywood Broun

Gawaine Le Coeur-Hardy was the worst pupil at knight school. He was tall and strong, but he didn't have much spirit. He would hide in the woods when the jousting class was called. His friends and teachers would shout to him to come out and break his neck like a man. Even when they told him that the lances were padded, the horses no more than ponies, and the field soft, Gawaine would not come. The Principal and the Assistant Principal were talking about Gawaine one spring afternoon. The Assistant Principal thought Gawaine should be kicked out of school.

"No," said the Principal, "I think I'll train him to slay dragons."

"He might be killed," said the Assistant Principal.

"So he might," replied the Principal happily. But he added, "We must think about the greater good."

"Are the dragons bad this year?" interrupted the Assistant Principal.

"I've never known them worse," replied the Principal. "Up in the hills to the south last week they killed a number of farmers, two cows, and a prize pig. And if this dry spell holds there's no telling when they may start a forest fire simply by

breathing around. Before I send Gawaine up in the hills I'm going to give him a magic word."

"That's a good idea," said the Assistant Principal. "Sometimes they work wonders."

From that day on Gawaine studied about dragons. In the morning there were long lectures on the history, manners, and customs of dragons. Gawaine did not do well in these studies. In the afternoon he did better, for then he would go down to the South Meadow and practice with a battle-ax. He had great strength as well as speed and grace. It was a thrilling sight to see Gawaine charging across the field toward the dummy paper dragon which had been set up for his practice. As he ran he would swing his ax and shout, "A murrain on thee!" or some other bit of school slang. It never took him more than one stroke to behead the dummy dragon.

Slowly his task was made more difficult. Paper gave way to wood, but even the toughest of these dummy dragons had no terrors for Gawaine. One sweep of the ax always did the business. The Principal decided by the end of June that it was time for the test. Only the night before, a dragon had come close to the school grounds and had eaten some of the lettuce from the garden. The teachers decided that Gawaine was ready. They gave him a diploma and a new battle-ax and the Principal called him to his office.

"Sit down," said the Principal. "You are no longer a boy. You are a man. Tomorrow you will go out into the world. Life is a matter of facts. It calls on the young and the old alike to face these facts, even though they are hard. Your problem, for example, is to slay dragons."

"They say that those dragons down in the South Wood are five hundred feet long," said Gawaine, trembling a little.

"Stuff and nonsense!" said the Principal. "A teacher saw one last week from the top of Arthur's Hill. The dragon was sunning himself down in the valley. The teacher didn't have a chance to look at him very long because he felt it was his duty to hurry back to make a report to me. He said the monster—or shall I say, the big lizard—wasn't an inch over two hundred feet. But the size has nothing at all to do with it. You'll find the big ones even easier than the little ones. They're far slower on their feet and less brave, I'm told. Besides, before you go I'm going to give you something. Then you need have no fear of all the dragons in the world."

"I'd like a magic cap," said Gawaine. "A cap to make me disappear."

The Principal laughed. "You mustn't believe all those old stories," he said. "There isn't any such thing. A cap to make you disappear, indeed! What would you do with it? You haven't even appeared yet. Why, my boy, you could walk from here to New York, and nobody would so much as look at you. You're nobody. You couldn't be more invisible than that. Don't worry; I'll give you something much better than an enchanted cap. I'm going to give you a magic word. All you have to do is to repeat this magic charm once and no dragon can possibly harm a hair of your head. You can cut off his head easily."

He took a heavy book from the shelf behind his desk and began to run through it. "Sometimes," he said, "the charm is a whole phrase or even a sentence. But I think a single word would be best for dragons."

"A short word," suggested Gawaine.

"It can't be too short. There isn't so much hurry as all that. Here's a fine magic word: 'Rumplesnitz.' Do you think you can learn that?"

Gawaine tried and in an hour or so he seemed to have the word down pat. Again and again he interrupted the lesson to ask, "And if I say 'Rumplesnitz' the dragon can't possibly hurt me?" And always the Principal replied, "If you only say 'Rumplesnitz,' you are perfectly safe."

The Principal saw him to the edge of the forest and pointed him to the direction in which he should travel. About a mile away to the southwest there was an open field in the woods. The Principal told Gawaine that under the steam he would find a dragon. Gawaine went forward slowly. He wondered whether it would be best to approach the dragon on the run, as he did in his practice in the South Meadow, or to walk slowly toward him, shouting "Rumplesnitz" all the way.

The problem was decided for him. No sooner had he come to the edge of the meadow than the dragon spied him and began to charge. It was a large dragon and yet it seemed brave in spite of what the Principal had said. As the dragon charged, it let out huge clouds of hissing steam through its nose. It was almost as if a huge teapot had gone crazy. The dragon came forward so fast and Gawaine was so frightened that he had time to say "Rumplesnitz" only once. As he said it, he swung his battle-ax and off popped the head of the dragon. Gawaine had to admit that it was even easier to kill a real dragon than a wooden one if only you said "Rumplesnitz."

Gawaine brought the ears home and a small part of the tail. His schoolmates and the teachers made much of him, but the Principal wisely kept him from being spoiled by insisting that he go on with his work. Every clear day Gawaine rose at dawn and went out to kill dragons. The Principal kept him at home when it rained, because he said the woods were damp and unhealthy at such times and he didn't want the boy to run needless risks. Few good days passed in which Gawaine failed to get a dragon. One day he killed three, a husband and wife and a visiting relative. Slowly he developed a method. Pupils who sometimes watched him from the hilltops a long way off said that he often allowed the dragon to come within a few feet before he said "Rumplesnitz." He came to say it with a mocking sneer. Now and then he did stunts. Once he went into action with his right hand tied behind his back. The dragon's head came off just as easily.

As Gawaine's record of killings mounted higher the Principal found it impossible to keep him completely in hand. He fell into the habit of stealing out at night and drinking at the village tavern. It was after such a party that he rose a little before dawn one fine August morning and started out after his fiftieth dragon. His head was heavy and his mind sluggish. He was heavy in other ways as well, for he had the habit of wearing his medals, ribbons and all, when he went out dragon hunting. The medals began on his chest and ran all the way down to his stomach. They must have weighed at least eight pounds.

Gawaine found a dragon in the same field where he had killed the first one. It was a fair-sized dragon, but an old one. Its face was wrinkled and Gawaine thought he had never seen so ugly a face. Much to the lad's disgust, the monster refused to charge. Gawaine had to walk toward him. He whistled as he went. The dragon watched hopelessly. Of course it had heard of Gawaine. Even when the lad raised his battle-ax the dragon made no move. It knew that there was no hope, for it had been told that this hunter was protected by magic. It waited, hoping something would turn up. Gawaine raised the battle-ax and suddenly lowered it again. He had grown very pale and he trembled. The dragon thought it was a trick. "What's the matter?" it asked.

"I've forgotten the magic word," stammered Gawaine.

"What a pity," said the dragon. "So that was the secret. It doesn't seem quite sporting to me, all this magic stuff, you know."

Gawaine was so helpless with terror that the dragon decided to show off a bit.

"Could I be of any help?" it asked. "What's the first letter of the magic word?"

"It begins with an 'r,'" said Gawaine weakly.

"Let's see," said the dragon, "that doesn't tell us much, does it?"

Gawaine shook his head.

"Well, then," said the dragon, "we'd better get down to business. Will you surrender?"

Gawaine got up enough courage to speak.

"What will you do if I surrender?" he asked.

"Why, I'll eat you," said the dragon.

"And if I don't surrender?"

"I'll eat you just the same."

"Then it doesn't make any difference, does it?" moaned Gawaine.

"It does to me," said the dragon with a smile. "I'd rather you didn't surrender. You'd taste much better if you didn't."

Then the dragon drew back his head and struck. In that second there flashed into the mind of Gawaine the magic word "Rumplesnitz," but there was no time to say it. There was time only to strike and, without a word, Gawaine met the onrush of the dragon with a full swing. He put all his back and shoulders into it. The head of the dragon flew away almost a hundred yards and landed in a bush.

Gawaine did not remain frightened very long after the death of the dragon. But he was puzzled. He cut off the ears of the monster almost in a daze. Again and again he thought to himself, "I didn't say 'Rumplesnitz'!" He was sure of that and yet there was no question that he had killed the dragon. In fact, he had never killed one better. Never before had he driven a head for anything like the same distance. All the way back to the knight school he kept rumbling about in his mind seeking a reason for what had happened. He went to the Principal and after closing the door told him what had happened. "I didn't say 'Rumplesnitz'," he explained.

The Principal laughed. "I'm glad you've found out," he said. "It makes you ever so much more of a hero. Don't you see that! Now you know that it was you who killed all these dragons and not that foolish little word 'Rumplesnitz'."

Gawaine frowned. "Then it wasn't a magic word after all?" he asked.

"Of course not," said the Principal; "you ought to be too old for such foolishness. There isn't any such thing as a magic word."

"But you told me it was magic," said Gawaine. "You said it was magic and now you say it isn't."

"It wasn't magic," answered the Principal, "but it was much more wonderful than that. The word gave you courage. It took away your fears. If I hadn't told you that, you might have been killed the very first time. It was your battle-ax did the trick."

Gawaine was bothered by the explanation. "If I hadn't of hit 'em all mighty hard and fast any one of 'em might have crushed me like a, like a—" He fumbled for a word.

"Eggshell," suggested the Principal.

"Like a eggshell," said Gawaine, and he said it many times. All through the evening meal people who sat near him heard him muttering, "Like a eggshell, like a eggshell."

The next day was clear, but Gawaine did not get up at dawn. Indeed, it was almost noon when the Principal found him in bed, with the sheet pulled over his head. The Principal called the Assistant Principal and together they dragged the boy toward the forest.

"He'll be all right as soon as he gets a couple more dragons under his belt," explained the Principal.

The Assistant Principal agreed. "It would be a shame to stop such a fine run," he said. "Why, counting that one yesterday, he's killed fifty dragons."

Now it's time for YOU to be The Reader as Detective.

What do you think will happen when Gawaine faces his next dragon? Read on to see if you are right.

They pushed the boy into a bush above which hung a small cloud of steam. It was quite a small dragon. But Gawaine did not come back that night or the next. In fact, he never came back. Some weeks afterward brave pupils from the school went into the bush, but they could find nothing to remind them of Gawaine except the metal parts of his medals. Even the ribbons had been eaten.

The Principal and the Assistant Principal agreed that it would be just as well not to tell the school how Gawaine had made his record and still less how he came to die. They held that it might be bad for school spirit. So, Gawaine has lived in the memory of the school as its greatest hero. No visitor succeeds in leaving the building today without seeing a great shield which hangs on the wall of the dining hall. Fifty pairs of dragons' ears are mounted upon the shield and underneath in gilt letters is "Gawaine le Coeur-Hardy," followed by the simple inscription, "He killed fifty dragons." The record has never been equaled.

I. The Reader as Detective

Read each of the following questions. Then write the letter of the correct answer to each question. Remember, the symbol next to each question identifies the *kind* of reading skill that particular question helps you to develop.

1. The Principal gave Gawaine
   a. an ax.
   b. a cap to make him disappear.
   c. a magic word.

2. Which of the following is true of Gawaine?

   a. He had great strength.
   b. He had lots of spirit.
   c. He did well in his studies.

3. We may infer that

   a. Gawaine looked forward to fighting the fifty-first dragon.
   b. Gawaine was too frightened to kill the fifty-first dragon.
   c. the fifty-first dragon was the most powerful dragon that Gawaine had ever faced.

4. Gawaine's job was "to slay dragons." What is the meaning of the word *slay*?

   a. trick   *b.* kill   *c.* teach

5. Gawaine defeated the fiftieth dragon

   a. without saying "Rumplesnitz."
   b. with the help of the word "Rumplesnitz."
   c. by scaring it to death.

6. This story makes the point that

   a. everyone should believe in magic words.
   b. dragons are not as dangerous as they appear to be.
   c. confidence can be as important as ability.

7. The word "Rumplesnitz" was important to Gawaine because

   a. it gave him courage.
   b. it kept dragons from seeing him.
   c. it made the dragons weak.

8. After the Principal told Gawaine that "There isn't any such thing as a magic word," Gawaine

   a. received a diploma and a new battle-ax.
   b. started out after his fiftieth dragon.
   c. stayed in bed with the sheet pulled over his head.

9. Gawaine listened to "lectures on the history, manners, and customs of dragons." Which of the following best defines the word *lectures*?

   a. teachers   *b.* books   *c.* talks

10. Suppose this story appeared as a news article in a newspaper. Which of the following would make the best headline?

   a. The Truth About a Great Hero
   b. Dragons Worse Than Ever This Year
   c. Teachers Wonder What to Do About Gawaine

II. On the Trail

DISCERNING CHARACTER

You are aware that by recognizing, or *discerning*, character you will more fully understand and appreciate what you are reading. In "The Fifty-First Dragon," for example, the author's characterization of Gawaine plays a critical, or highly important, part in the story.

Answer the following questions. Each one deals with the characterization of Gawaine.

11. Gawaine was swift and strong; he was also

   a. a coward.   *c.* clumsy and awkward in battle.
   b. very brave.

12. Evidence found in the story suggests that Gawaine was

   a. not very tall.   *c.* very bright.
   b. not especially smart.

13. Which of the following shows that Gawaine was proud?

   a. He wore eight pounds of ribbons when he went hunting dragons.
   b. He became helpless with terror when he forgot the magic word.
   c. He hid in the woods when the jousting class began.

14. Which of the following statements is correct?

   a. Gawaine was too slow and weak to kill dragons, so he needed a magic word.
   b. Gawaine could not believe that he, rather than the magic word, had killed the dragons.
   c. After a while, Gawaine realized that he had the ability to kill dragons.

15. It is fair to say that Gawaine did not

    a. have confidence in himself.

    b. believe in the power of magic words.

    c. have the skill to kill dragons.

III. Finding Word Meanings

The ten words listed below appear in "The Fifty-First Dragon." Study the words and their definitions. Then complete the following paragraphs by using each vocabulary word only *once*.

		page
invisible	not able to be seen	113
enchanted	magic	113
mocking	making fun of	114
sneer	look intended to make one feel low or worthless	114
stunts	acts that draw attention	114
sluggish	slow moving	114
stammered	spoke slowly and haltingly because of nervousness	115
daze	state of being unable to think clearly	115
shame	feeling of disgrace; pity	116
inscription	written words	117

With an unpleasant __16__ on its face, the dragon studied me closely. "What are you doing in this magical, __17__ forest?" it demanded. These woods are for dragons only! Being here should make you feel dishonor and __18__ !"

Oh, how I wished I were __19__ at the moment, so that no one could see me. I wanted to run, but I suddenly felt lazy and __20__ .

"I—I—I seem to have lost my way," I __21__ . "I didn't see the sign with the __22__ , 'Keep Out'!"

"Are you __23__ me by making fun of what I say?" the dragon exclaimed. "You must be punished now for your foolish pranks and __24__ !"

Roaring loudly, the dragon filled the air with flames. Just then, I awoke. But for the following hour, I remained lost in a foggy __25__ .

IV. Reviewing the Case

Now it's time to review the case. In a paragraph, explain what you think the Principal's plan was when he gave Gawaine the magic word. Then, in another paragraph, explain why the Principal's plan didn't work.

Afterwards, discuss what lesson or lessons the story teaches.

August Heat

by W. F. Harvey

PHENISTONE ROAD, CLAPHAM
August 20th, 1905

I have had what I believe to be the most remarkable day in my life. Now, while the events are still fresh in my mind, I wish to put them down on paper as clearly as possible

Let me say at once that my name is James Clarence Withencroft. I am forty-five years old, in perfect health. I have never known a day's illness.

I am an artist, not a very successful one. But I earn enough money by my drawings to satisfy my needs.

My only near relative, a sister, died five years ago, so that I am quite alone.

I ate breakfast this morning at nine. After glancing through the morning paper, I lighted my pipe and let my mind wander. I hoped that I might think of some subject to draw.

The room, though the door and windows were open, was unbelievably hot. I had just made up my mind to go to the neighborhood swimming pool, when an idea for a drawing came to me.

I began to work. So intent was I on my drawing that I left my lunch untouched. I finally stopped working when the clock struck four. The result, for a hurried sketch, was, I felt sure, the best thing I had done.

It showed a criminal in court right after the judge had pronounced sentence. The man was fat—enormously fat. The flesh hung in rolls around his chin. It wrinkled his huge, thick neck. He was clean-shaven and almost bald. He stood there, looking straight in front of him, his short, clumsy fingers clutching the rail. The feeling that his expression conveyed was not so much one of horror. It was as though he was completely exhausted.

I rolled up my sketch. Without quite knowing why, I placed it in my pocket. Then, with the feeling of happiness a thing done well gives, I left the house.

I believe that I set out with the idea of calling upon my friend, Trenton. For I remember walking along Lytton Street and turning to the right along Gilchrist Road.

From there on, I have only the vaguest memory of where

I went. The one thing I was aware of was the terrible heat. It came up from the street almost in waves. I longed for the thunder promised by the clouds that hung low over the western sky.

I must have walked five or six miles, when a small boy woke me from my dream-like state. He asked me the time.

It was twenty minutes to seven.

When he left me, I began to become aware of where I was. I found myself standing in front of a gate that led into a yard. Above the entrance was a board with these words:

CHARLES ATKINSON
MONUMENTS MADE
I WORK IN ENGLISH AND ITALIAN MARBLE

From the yard itself came a cheery whistle, the noise of hammer blows, and the cold sound of steel meeting stone.

Something made me enter.

A man was sitting with his back toward me. He was busy at work on a slab of marble. He turned around as he heard my steps.

It was the man I had been drawing. His picture was in my pocket.

He sat there, huge, enormous, the sweat pouring from his scalp, which he wiped with a handkerchief. But though the face was the same, the expression was completely different.

He greeted me smiling, as if we were old friends. He shook my hand.

I said I was sorry for breaking in on him.

"Everything is hot and glary outside," I said. "This is like an oasis in the desert."

"I don't know about the oasis," he replied. "But it certainly is hot! Take a seat, sir."

He pointed to the end of the gravestone on which he was at work. I sat down.

"That's a beautiful stone you're working on," I said.

He shook his head. "In a way it is," he answered. "The surface here is as fine as anything you might want. But there's a crack at the back, though I don't think you'd notice it. I could never do a really good job with a piece of marble like that. It would be all right in the summer. It wouldn't mind this blasted heat. But wait until the winter comes. It would break. There's nothing like frost to find the weak spots in stone."

"Then what's it for?" I asked.

The man burst out laughing.

"It's for a show. That's the truth. Artists have shows. We have them, too. All the latest little things in headstones, you know."

He went on to talk about marble. He spoke of which kind stood up best to wind and rain. He spoke of which were easiest to cut. Then he talked about his garden and his flowers. Every minute or so, he would drop his tools, wipe his shining head, and curse the heat.

I said little, for I felt uneasy. There was something unnatural, strange, in meeting this man.

I tried at first to tell myself that I had seen him before—that his face had been buried in some out-of-the-way corner of my memory. But I knew that I was only fooling myself.

Mr. Atkinson finished his work. He got up with a sigh of relief.

"There! What do you think of that?" he said proudly.

I looked at the words which he had carved into the stone. They said—

TO THE MEMORY OF
JAMES CLARENCE WITHENCROFT.
BORN JANUARY 18TH, 1860
HE PASSED AWAY VERY SUDDENLY
ON AUGUST 20TH, 1905

For some time I sat in silence. Then a cold shudder ran down my spine. I asked him where he had seen the name.

"Oh, I didn't see it anywhere," replied Mr. Atkinson. "I wanted some name. So I put down the first one that came into my head. Why do you want to know?"

"It's a strange coincidence, but it happens to be my name."

He gave a long, low whistle. "And the dates?"

"I can only answer for one of them—and that's correct."

"It's a strange thing," he said.

I told him of my morning's work. I took the sketch from my pocket and showed it to him. As he looked, the expression on his face began to change. It became more and more like that of the man I had drawn.

"You probably heard my name," I said.

"And you must have seen me somewhere and forgotten it! Were you at Clacton* last July?"

I had never been to Clacton in my life. We were silent for some time. We were both looking at the same thing—the two dates on the gravestone, and the first one was right!

"Come inside and have some supper," said Mr. Atkinson.

His wife was a cheerful woman. Atkinson introduced me as a friend of his who was an artist. After supper, Atkinson and I went outside. He sat on the gravestone.

"You must excuse me for asking," I said. "But have you done anything for which you could be put on trial?"

He shook his head and said, "No."

Atkinson got up. He took a can from the porch and began to water the flowers. "I do this twice a day in the hot weather," he said. "Even then the heat sometimes is too much for the weak ones. Where do you live?"

I told him my address. It would take an hour's quick walk to get back home.

"It's like this," he said. "Let's look at the matter carefully. If you go back home tonight, there's always a chance of an accident. You might get run over, or fall—anything could happen."

He spoke of things very unlikely, things I would have laughed at six hours before. But I did not laugh.

"The best thing to do," he continued, "is for you to stay here until twelve o'clock. We'll go upstairs and relax. It may be cooler inside."

To my surprise I agreed.

We were sitting in a long, low room. Atkinson's wife has gone to bed. He is busy sharpening some tools at a little grindstone.

The air seems charged with thunder. I am writing this at a shaky table in front of the open window. The leg is cracked. Atkinson, who is a handy man with his tools, is going to fix it as soon as he has put a sharp edge on his chisel.

It is after eleven now. I shall be gone in less than an hour.

---

*A seaside resort in England.

But the heat is unbearable.
It is enough to make a man mad.

> Now it's time for YOU to be The Reader as Detective.
>
> "August Heat" seems to end at this point. But the story actually continues—in your imagination. What do you think will happen *now*? Think back to the drawing and the gravestone. Read the last four paragraphs of the story again. What is going to happen, Reader as Detective?

I. The Reader as Detective

Read each of the following questions. Then write the letter of the correct answer to each question. Remember, the symbol next to each question identifies the *kind* of reading skill that particular question helps you to develop.

1. James Clarence Withencroft was

   a. an artist.   *c.* a famous writer.

   b. a stonecutter.

2. Which group of words best describes the man in the drawing?

   a. clean-shaven, thin, nearly bald

   b. clean-shaven, fat, tired

   c. thick neck, clumsy fingers, heavy beard

3. We may infer that

   a. Withencroft returned home after twelve o'clock.

   b. Withencroft had an accident on his way home.

   c. Atkinson killed Withencroft.

4. This story takes place

   a. on a hot day in August.   *c.* at Clacton in July.

   b. on January 18th, 1860.

5. Which one of the following happened after Atkinson and Withencroft ate supper?

   a. Withencroft walked along Lytton Street and then up Gilchrist Road.
   b. Atkinson discussed different kinds of marble.
   c. Withencroft went upstairs to relax.

6. Withencroft completed "a hurried sketch." Which of the following best defines the word *sketch*?

   a. rough drawing   *c.* artist's show
   b. headstone

7. Which of the following is true of Atkinson?

   a. He didn't mind the heat.
   b. He was not very handy.
   c. He looked like the man in the picture.

8. Which statement below expresses an opinion?

   a. I felt sure that the picture was the best thing I had done.
   b. I water the flowers twice a day in the hot weather.
   c. I am writing this at a shaky table in front of the open window.

9. Atkinson was busy putting "a sharp edge on his chisel." Which of the following expressions best defines the word *chisel* as used in this sentence?

   a. cheat or trick   *c.* sharp tool
   b. cut out or shape

10. This story is mainly about

   a. how a man takes a long walk on a very hot day.
   b. how strange events suggest that a man will be killed.
   c. the way to make headstones.

II. On the Trail

DRAWING CONCLUSIONS

You are aware that a good reader uses facts and story clues to *draw conclusions*. Few stories offer the reader more opportunities to practice this skill than "August Heat." It is truly a story which demands that the reader be a reading detective.

Answer each of the questions below. Think carefully about what happens in the story as you draw your conclusions.

11. We may conclude that Atkinson
   a. fixed the table and went straight to bed.
   b. helped Withencroft arrive home safely.
   c. killed Withencroft some time before midnight.

12. Probably, Atkinson was greatly affected by
   a. the fear that Withencroft would murder him.
   b. the unbearable heat which drove him mad.
   c. jealousy over Withencroft's wealth.

13. Evidence in the story leads us to guess that Withencroft was killed by
   a. a sharp chisel.   c. a bad fall.
   b. a heavy stone.

14. The picture that Withencroft drew suggests that
   a. he had never been in a courthouse.
   b. his murderer was caught and sentenced.
   c. Atkinson was never seen or heard from again.

15. There is reason to conclude that Withencroft
   a. was planning to become a stonecutter.
   b. later sold his paintings for much money.
   c. died on August 20th.

III. Finding Word Meanings

Following are five vocabulary words which appear in "August Heat" and five *new* vocabulary words for you to learn. Study the words and their definitions. Then complete the following paragraphs by using each vocabulary word only *once.*

		page
remarkable	unusual	122
intent	strong purpose; strongly fixed on something	122

		page
conveyed	given; gave	123
vaguest	slightest; very unclear	123
coincidence	the change happening of two things in such a way as to be striking or unusual	125
occurs	happens	
comprehend	understand	
former	the first of two	
varying	different; unlike	
member	person belonging to a group	

"August Heat" is one of the most __16__ stories ever written. Because of its unusual style, readers have different, or __17__ , reactions to it. Some readers understand and __18__ everything that __19__ in the story. They are able to grasp all that the author has __20__ . For these readers, the story has great power. Other, less careful readers have only the __21__ idea of what is happening. They are unable to understand the author's __22__ .

We trust that you, the reader as detective, are a __23__ of the __24__ group. Did you carefully think about the meaning of each striking and unusual __25__ in the story? Did you "get" what the author had in mind?

IV. Reviewing the Case

Now it's time to review the case. Explain how each of the following played an important part in "August Heat." Answer in a well-written paragraph for each.

A. The picture that Withencroft drew
B. The gravestone that Atkinson made
C. The terrible heat

Perhaps, later, you and your classmates will have an opportunity to share ideas about what happened to Withencroft.

Charles

by Shirley Jackson

The day my son Laurie started kindergarten, he gave up his little-boy clothes and began wearing blue jeans with a belt. I watched him go off that first morning with the older girl next door, looking as though he were going off to a fight.

He came home the same way at lunchtime. "Isn't anybody *here*?" he yelled. At the table, he knocked over his little sister's milk.

"How was school today?" I asked.

"Did you learn anything?"

"I didn't learn nothing," he said.

"*Anything*," I said. "Didn't learn *anything*."

"But the teacher spanked a boy," Laurie said, "for being fresh."

"What did he do?" I asked. "Who was it?"

Laurie thought. "It was Charles," he said. "The teacher spanked him and made him stand in the corner. He was really fresh."

"What did he do?" I asked. But Laurie slid off his chair, took a cookie, and left.

The next day, Laurie remarked at lunch, "Charles was bad again today." He grinned. "Today Charles hit the teacher," he said.

"Good heavens," I said. "I suppose he got spanked again?"

"He sure did," Laurie said.

131

"Why did Charles hit the teacher?" I asked.

"Because she tried to make him color with red crayons. Charles wanted to color with green crayons, so he hit the teacher. She spanked him and said nobody play with Charles, but everybody did."

The third day, Charles bounced a seesaw onto the head of a little girl and made her bleed. The teacher made him stay inside during recess.

On Thursday, Charles had to stand in a corner, because he was pounding his feet on the floor during story time. Friday, Charles could not use the blackboard because he threw chalk.

On Saturday, I talked to my husband about it. "Do you think kindergarten is too disturbing for Laurie?" I asked him. "This Charles boy sounds like a bad influence."

"It will be all right," my husband said. "There are bound to be people like Charles in the world. He might as well meet them now as later."

On Monday, Laurie came home late. "Charles!" he shouted, as he ran up to the house. "Charles was bad again!"

I let him in and helped him take off his coat. "You know what Charles did?" he demanded. "Charles yelled so much that the teacher came in from first grade. She said our teacher had to keep Charles quiet. And so Charles had to stay after school, and all the children stayed to watch him."

"What did he do?" I asked.

"He just sat there," Laurie said, noticing his father. "Hi, Pop, you old dust mop."

"What does this Charles look like?" my husband asked. "What's his last name?"

"He's bigger than me," Laurie said. "And he doesn't wear a jacket."

I could hardly wait for the first Parent-Teachers meeting. I wanted very much to meet Charles' mother. The meeting was still a week away.

On Tuesday, Laurie said, "Our teacher had a friend come to see her in school today."

My husband and I said together, "Was it Charles' mother?"

"Naaah," Laurie said. "It was a man who came and made us do exercises like this." He jumped off his chair and touched his toes. Then he sat down again. "Charles didn't even *do* exercises."

"Didn't he want to?" I asked.

"Naaah," Laurie said. "Charles was so fresh to the teacher's friend, they wouldn't *let* him do exercises."

"Fresh again?" I said.

"He kicked the teacher's friend," Laurie said. "The teacher's friend told Charles to touch his toes, and Charles kicked him."

"What do you think they'll do about Charles?" my husband asked.

"I don't know," Laurie said. "Throw him out of school, I guess."

Wednesday and Thursday were routine. Charles yelled during story time and hit a boy in the stomach and made him cry. On Friday, Charles stayed after school again, and so did all the other children.

On Monday of the third week, Laurie came home with another report. "You know what Charles did today?" he demanded. "He told a girl to say a word, and she said it. The teacher washed her mouth out with soap, and Charles laughed."

"What word?" his father asked.

"It's so bad, I'll have to whisper it to you," Laurie said, and whispered into my husband's ear.

"Charles told the little girl to say *that*?" he said, his eyes widening.

"She said it *twice*," Laurie said. "Charles told her to say it *twice*."

"What happened to Charles?" my husband asked.

"Nothing," Laurie said. "He was passing out the crayons."

The next day, Charles said the evil word himself three or four times, and got his mouth washed out with soap each time. He also threw chalk.

My husband came to the door that night as I was leaving for the Parent-Teachers meeting. "Invite her over after the meeting," he said. "I want to get a look at the mother of that kid."

"I hope she's there," I said.

"She'll be there," my husband said. "How could they hold a Parent-Teachers meeting without Charles' mother?"

At the meeting, I looked over the faces of all the other mothers. None of them looked unhappy enough to be the mother of Charles. No one stood up and apologized for the way her son had been acting. No one mentioned Charles.

After the meeting I found Laurie's teacher. "I've been so anxious to meet you," I said. "I'm Laurie's mother."

"Oh, yes," she said. "We're all so interested in Laurie."

"He certainly likes kindergarten," I said. "He talks about it all the time."

"He's had some trouble getting used to school," she said, "but I think he'll be all right."

"Laurie usually adjusts quickly," I said. "I suppose his trouble might be from Charles' influence."

"Charles?" the teacher said.

"Yes," I said, laughing. "You must have your hands full with Charles."

> Now it's time for YOU to be The Reader as Detective.
>
> What do you think Laurie's teacher answered? Read on to see if you are right.

"Charles?" she said. "We don't have any Charles in the kindergarten."

I. The Reader as Detective

Read each of the following questions. Then write the letter of the correct answer to each question. Remember, the symbol next to each question identifies the *kind* of reading skill that particular question helps you to develop.

1. When Laurie started kindergarten, he began wearing
a. little-boy clothes.   *c.* blue jeans.
b. a shirt and a tie.

2. The teacher spanked Charles because he
a. came to school late.
b. was fresh.
c. never did his homework.

3. We many infer that Charles
a. sometimes walked home with Laurie.
b. was a very good student.
c. was Laurie.

4. Laurie's mother told the teacher, "I've been so anxious to meet you." As used in this sentence, the word *anxious* means
a. eager.   *b.* worried.   *c.* terrified.

5. Which of the following is correct?
a. Laurie seldom spoke about school.
b. Laurie often spoke about school.
c. Laurie got used to school right away.

6. The story is told by

    a. Charles.   *c.* Laurie's mother.

    b. Laurie.

7. Which of the following statements is a fact?

    a. Charles was bigger than Laurie, and didn't wear a jacket.

    b. Kindergarten is more important than any other grade.

    c. Laurie's teacher said that they were all interested in Laurie.

8. Which happened first?

    a. Charles refused to do exercises.

    b. Laurie said that Charles got spanked in school.

    c. Laurie's mother went to the Parent-Teachers meeting.

9. Laurie's mother expected Charles' mother to be

    a. very happy.

    b. well dressed.

    c. upset about Charles.

10. This story is mainly about

    a. the adventures of a boy called Charles.

    b. what children learn in kindergarten.

    c. what happened at a Parent-Teachers meeting.

II. On the Trail

DISCERNING CHARACTER

Answer the following questions. Each one deals with *characterization* in "Charles."

11. Which word best describes Charles?

    a. helpful   *b.* friendly   *c.* wild

12. Which sentence best characterizes Laurie?

    a. He was quiet and shy.

    b. He was very high-spirited.

    c. He always listened to his teacher.

13. Laurie's mother was

    a. very interested in how Laurie was doing at school.

    b. not too interested in how Laurie was doing at school.

    c. surprised at how well Laurie was doing at school.

14. Which of the following is true of Laurie?

    a. He was often absent from school.

    b. He never got into fights.

    c. He had trouble getting used to kindergarten.

15. At the end of the story, Laurie's mother probably felt

    a. shocked and surprised.

    b. pleased and delighted.

    c. proud of Laurie.

III. Finding Word Meanings

Listed below are five vocabulary words which appear in "Charles" and five *new* vocabulary words for you to learn. Study the words and their definitions. Then complete the following paragraphs by using each vocabulary word only *once*.

		page
disturbing	upsetting	132
influence	having an effect on others	132
routine	usual; average	133
apologized	offered an excuse; said one is sorry	134
adjusts	gets used to	134
indicate	show; say	
flustered	mixed up	
effectively	with skill or ability	
initial	earliest; first	
anticipated	expected	

Do you remember your first, or __16__, day at school? Did things happen as you thought or __17__ that they would? Were you comfortable and at ease, or did you find the new experience bewildering and __18__?

Chances are you were a little frightened at the change from the ordinary and __19__ . But with the help of your teachers who had a good __20__ on you, you probably soon settled down.

Everyone __21__ to new situations differently. Some people handle them well and __22__ . Others, however, become nervous and __23__ . Sometimes they say or do things which are embarrassing. If this should happen to you, just __24__ that you are sorry. After you have __25__ , you will begin to feel better.

IV. Reviewing the Case

Now it's time to review the case.

A. In two or three paragraphs, describe Charles. Use *incidents*, or examples, from the story to show the kind of person he is.

B. In two or three paragraphs, describe Laurie. Use incidents from the story to support your point of view.

Raymond's Run

by Toni Cade Bambara

I don't have much work to do around the house like some girls. My mother does that. And I don't have to earn pocket money. My brother George runs errands for the big boys and sells Christmas cards. And anything else that's got to get done, my father does. All I have to do in life is mind my brother Raymond, which is enough.

He's much bigger than me and he's older too. But a lot of people call him my little brother because he's not quite right and needs a lot of looking after. And if anybody tries to tease him, they have to deal with me. And I don't believe in standing round doing a lot of talking. I'd rather just knock you down and take my chances, even if I am a little girl with skinny arms and a squeaky voice, which is how I got the name Squeaky. And if things get too rough, I run. And as anybody can tell you, I'm the fastest thing on two feet.

There is no track meet where I don't win the first-place medal. I used to win the twenty-yard dash when I was a little kid in kindergarten. Nowadays it's the fifty-yard dash. I'm the swiftest thing in the neighborhood. Everybody knows that— except two people who know better, my father and me.

He can beat me to Amsterdam Avenue with me getting a good head start and him running with his hands in his pockets, whistling. But that's private information. 'Cause can you imagine some thirty-five-year-old man stuffing himself into running shorts to race little kids? So as far as everyone's concerned, I'm the fastest. That goes for Gretchen too. She has

139

put out the tale that she is going to win the first-place medal this year. Ridiculous. No one can beat me, and that's all there is to it.

I like to stroll down Broadway practicing my breathing exercises. I keep Raymond on the inside close to the building because he sometimes has fits of fantasy and starts thinking he's a circus performer and that the curb is a tightrope strung high in the air. Or sometimes if you don't watch him, he'll dash across traffic and start chasing pigeons. So I keep Raymond on the inside of me, and he plays like he's driving a stagecoach. That is okay with me as long as he doesn't run me over or interrupt my breathing exercises, which I have to do on account of I'm serious about my running and don't care who knows it.

Now, some people like to act like things come easy to them, won't let on that they practice. Not me. You can see me any time of day practicing running. I never walk if I can trot, and Raymond always keeps up because if he hangs back someone's liable to walk up to him and get smart, or take his allowance from him. People act so stupid sometimes.

So I'm strolling down Broadway breathing out and breathing in on counts of seven which is my lucky number. And here comes Gretchen and her two sidekicks. One is Mary Louise, who used to be a friend of mine when she first moved to Harlem from Baltimore. The other is Rosie, who is as fat as I am skinny, and makes fun of Raymond all the time. She is too stupid to know that there is not a great deal of difference between herself and Raymond, so who is she to throw stones.

So they are coming up Broadway, and I see right away that it's going to be one of those Dodge City scenes 'cause the street ain't that big and they're close to the buildings just as we are. First I think I'll step into the candy store and let them pass. But that's chicken, and I've got a reputation to consider. So then I think I'll just walk straight on through them or over them if necessary. But as they get to me, they slow down. I'm ready to fight if I have to, 'cause, like I said, I don't feature a whole lot of chitchat.

"You signing up for the May Day races?" smiles Mary Louise, only it's not really a smile.

A dumb question like that doesn't deserve an answer.

"I don't think you're going to win this time," says Rosie, with her hands on her hips.

"I always win 'cause I'm the best," I say straight at Gretchen. Gretchen smiles, but it's not a real smile, it's fake. Then they all look at Raymond, who has just brought his make-believe mule team to a halt. And they're about to see what kind of trouble they can make for him.

"What grade you in now, Raymond?" asks Mary Louise.

"You got anything to say to him, say it to me, Mary Louise Williams."

"What are you, his mother?" says Rosie.

"That's right, Fatso. And one more word out of anybody and there'll be big trouble."

So they just stand there. Gretchen puts her hands on her hips and is about to say something but doesn't. Then she walks around me, looking me up and down, but keeps walking up Broadway, and her sidekicks follow her. So me and Raymond smile at each other, and he says "Gidyap" to his mule team, and I continue with my breathing exercises.

I take my time getting to the park on May Day because the track meet is the last thing on the program. I put Raymond in the swings. It's a tight squeeze this year and will be impossible next year. Then I look around for Mr. Pearson, who pins the numbers on. I'm really looking for Gretchen, if you want to know the truth. But she's not around. The park is jam-packed. There are parents in hats and kids in white dresses and light-blue suits. The big guys with their caps on backwards are leaning against the fence, swirling the basketballs on the tips of their fingers, waiting for all these crazy people to clear out so they can play.

Then here comes Mr. Pearson with a clipboard and his cards and pencils and whistles and safety pins and fifty million other things he's always dropping all over the place.

"Hello, Squeaky," he says, checking my name off the list and handing me number seven and a safety pin.

"Hazel Elizabeth Deborah Parker," I correct him and tell him to write it down on his board.

"Well, Hazel Elizabeth Deborah, are you going to give

someone else a chance this year?" I stare at him real hard to see if he is seriously thinking I should lose the race on purpose just to give someone else a break.

"There are only six girls running this time," he continues, shaking his head sadly like it's my fault all of New York didn't turn out in sneakers. "That new girl should give you a run for your money." He looks around the park for Gretchen like a periscope in a submarine movie. Then he says, "Wouldn't it be a nice gesture if you were . . . to ahhh . . ."

I give him such a look he couldn't finish putting that idea into words. Grown-ups got a lot of nerve sometimes. I pin number seven to myself and stomp away, I'm so burnt. And I go straight for the track and stretch out on the grass.

The twenty-yard dash is first. It takes all of two minutes 'cause most of the little kids don't know any better than to run off the track or run the wrong way or run smack into the fence and fall down and cry. Then comes the thirty-yard dash. I don't even bother to turn my head to watch 'cause Raphael Perez always wins. He is very fast, almost as fast as I am. After that is the forty-yard dash.

Raymond is hollering from the swings 'cause he knows I'm about to do my thing 'cause the man on the loudspeaker has just announced the fifty-yard dash. I get up and slip off my sweat pants, and then I see Gretchen standing at the starting line. She's kicking her legs out like a pro. Then as I get into place, I see that ole Raymond is in line on the other side of the fence. He's bending down, with his fingers on the ground, just like he knew what he was doing. I was going to yell at him, but then I didn't. It burns up your energy to holler.

Every time, just before I take off in a race, I always feel like I'm in a dream, the kind of dream you have when you're sick with fever and feel all hot and weightless. I dream I'm flying over a sandy beach in the early morning, kissing the leaves of the trees as I fly by. And there's always the smell of apples, just like in the country when I was little and used to think I was a choochoo train, running through the fields of corn and chugging up the hill to the orchard. And all the time I'm dreaming this, I get lighter and lighter until I'm flying over the beach again, getting blown through the sky like a feather that weighs nothing at all.

But once I spread my fingers in the dirt and crouch over for the Get on Your Mark, the dream is gone, and I am solid again and am telling myself, "Squeaky, you must win, you must win. You are the fastest thing in the world. You can even beat your father if you really try."

And then I feel my weight coming back just behind my knees, then down to my feet, then into the earth, and the pistol shot explodes in my blood, and I am off and weightless again. I'm flying past the other runners, my arms pumping up and down, and the whole world is quiet except for the crunch as I zoom over the gravel in the track.

I glance to my left and there is no one. To the right is Gretchen, who's got her chin jutting out as if it could win the race all by itself. And on the other side of the fence is Raymond, with his arms down to his side and the palms tucked up behind him, running in his very own style.

It's the first time I ever saw that, and I almost stop to watch my brother Raymond on his first run. But the white ribbon is heading toward me, and I tear past it, racing into the distance till my feet finally brake me short. Then all the kids standing on the side pile on me. They bang me on the back and slap my head with their May Day programs, for they think I have won again, and everybody on 151st Street can walk tall for another year.

"In first place . . ." says the man on the loudspeaker. But then he pauses, and the loudspeaker starts to whine. There is static and more noise. And I lean down to catch my breath, and here comes Gretchen, walking back. She's overshot the finish line too. She's huffing and puffing with her hands on her hips, taking it slow, breathing in steady time like a real pro. And I sort of like her a little for the first time.

"In first place . . ." says the man on the loudspeaker again. And then three or four voices get all mixed up in the loudspeaker, and I dig my sneaker into the grass and stare at Gretchen, who's staring back. We are both wondering just who did win. I can hear Mr. Pearson arguing with the man on the loudspeaker.

Then I hear Raymond yanking at the fence to call me, and I wave to shush him. But he keeps rattling the fence. Then, like a dancer or something, he starts climbing over it nice and easy but very fast. And it occurs to me watching, how

smoothly he climbs hand over hand. And I remember how he looked running with his arms down to his side.

> Now it's time for YOU to be The Reader as Detective.
>
> What do you think Squeaky suddenly realized as she watched Raymond? And what do you think she plans to *do* about her discovery? Read on to see if you are right.

It occurred to me that Raymond would make a very fine runner. Doesn't he always keep up with me on my runs? And he surely knows how to breathe in counts of seven 'cause he's always doing it at the dinner table.

And I'm smiling to beat the band 'cause if I've lost this race, or if me and Gretchen tied, or even if I've won, I can always retire as a runner and begin a whole new career as a coach with Raymond as my champion.

So I stand there with my new plan. And I'm laughing out loud by this time, as Raymond jumps down from the fence and runs over with his arms down at the side in his very own running style. And by the time he comes over, I'm jumping up and down, so glad to see him—my brother Raymond, a great runner in the family tradition.

But of course everyone thinks I'm jumping up and down because the man on the loudspeaker is announcing, "In first place—Miss Hazel Elizabeth Deborah Parker. In second place—Miss Gretchen P. Lewis."

And I look over at Gretchen, wondering what the **P** stands for. And I smile. 'Cause she's good, no doubt about it. Maybe she'd like to help me coach Raymond. Anyone can see she's obviously serious about running. And she nods to congratulate me, and then she smiles. And I smile. And we stand there with this big smile of respect between us. And it's for real.

I. The Reader as Detective

Read each of the following questions. Then write the letter of the correct answer to each question. Remember, the symbol next to each question identifies the *kind* of reading skill that particular question helps you to develop.

1. Squeaky's job was to

    a. sell Christmas cards.

    b. run errands.

    c. take care of Raymond.

2. Which of the following is true?

    a. Squeaky was a very fast runner.

    b. Squeaky could run faster than her father.

    c. Gretchen could run faster than Squeaky.

3. We may infer that the story takes place in

    a. New York.   *c.* Boston.

    b. Baltimore.

4. Which of the following happened last?

    a. Gretchen nodded and smiled at Squeaky.

    b. The man on the loudspeaker announced the fifty-yard dash.

    c. Rosie asked Raymond what grade he was in.

5. Gretchen was walking up the street with "her two sidekicks." The word *sidekicks* means

    a. close friends.   *c.* parents.

    b. enemies.

6. Squeaky's real name was

    a. Mary Louise.

    b. Hazel Elizabeth Deborah Parker.

    c. not given in the story.

7. According to Squeaky, "there is not a great deal of difference" between Rosie and Raymond. Squeaky was expressing

    a. a fact.   *c.* love for Rosie.

    b. an opinion.

8. Squeaky said that she didn't like making "a whole lot of chitchat." Which of the following means the same as *chitchat*?

    a. excuses   *c.* a kind of food
    b. small talk

9. Raymond sometimes thought that he was

    a. a circus performer.   *c.* both of the above.
    b. a stagecoach driver.

10. Which of the following would make the best title for the story?

    a. Squeaky's Run
    b. Gretchen Finishes Second
    c. How To Win a Race

II. On the Trail

DRAWING CONCLUSIONS

"Raymond's Run" is another story which provides the reader with opportunities to draw conclusions.

Answer the following questions. Think carefully about what happens in the story as you draw your conclusions.

11. It is correct to conclude that

    a. Raymond had the ability to be a fine runner.
    b. Raymond didn't like to watch Squeaky race.
    c. Squeaky will lose the next race she runs.

12. At the end of the story, Squeaky realized that

    a. she hated Gretchen.
    b. Gretchen wasn't too serious about running.
    c. coaching Raymond could be as satisfying as running.

13. When Squeaky saw Gretchen and Mary Louise coming up Broadway, she thought it was going to be "one of those Dodge City scenes." By this Squeaky meant that

    a. a big fight was coming up.
    b. they would all go to the movies.
    c. they were going to act in a play.

14. Squeaky probably thought that Mr. Pearson wanted her to

    a. win the race.

    b. finish last.

    c. let Gretchen win.

15. How do you think Squeaky felt at the conclusion of the story?

    a. proud and happy

    b. sad

    c. not too excited

III. Finding Word Meanings

The ten words listed below appear in "Raymond's Run." Study the words and their definitions. Then complete the following paragraphs by using each vocabulary word only *once*.

		page
ridiculous	deserving to be made fun of; laughable; silly	140
fantasy	a story that takes place in one's mind	140
liable	likely to	140
stroll	to walk slowly and easily	140
consider	think about; keep in mind	140
swirling	moving with a twisting motion	141
gesture	any movement or action that shows feeling	142
energy	strength or power	142
static	noises usually caused by electrical problems	143
congratulate	to show pleasure to someone who has been successful or lucky	145

Picture yourself as a great baseball player. The bases are filled as you slowly __16__ up to home plate. Over the noise of the __17__ of the loudspeaker, the announcer calls out your name. You tip your hat to the crowd—a __18__ everyone loves.

Is the pitcher __19__ to strike you out? You laugh to yourself. The thought is so silly and __20__ , you don't even __21__ it.

Now the ball is spinning and __22__ to you as you wait at home plate. Using all of your __23__ , you swing at the ball as hard as you can. After it sails high over the fence, you let all of your teammates shake your hand and __24__ you.

IV. Reviewing the Case

Now it's time to review the case. "Raymond's Run" is a story of *contrasts*, or differences. Use complete sentences to answer the following questions. Notice that each question deals with a contrast.

A. How does Squeaky treat Raymond? How do the other girls treat Raymond?

B. At the beginning of the story, how important is racing to Squeaky? How important is racing to Squeaky at the end of the story?

C. How do Gretchen and Squeaky feel about each other at the beginning of the story? How do they feel about each other at the end of the story?

The Chaser

by John Collier

Alan Austin, as nervous as a kitten, went up certain dark and creaky stairs in the neighborhood of Pell Street. He looked about for a long time on the dim landing before he found the name he wanted. It was written on one of the doors.

He pushed open this door as he had been told to do and found himself in a tiny room. It contained no furniture, just a plain kitchen table, a rocking chair, and an ordinary chair. On one of the dirty brown walls were a couple of shelves. On them were perhaps a dozen bottles and jars.

An old man sat in the rocking chair, reading a newspaper. Alan, without a word, handed him the card he had been given.

"Sit down, Mr. Austin," said the old man very politely. "I am glad to meet you."

"Is it true," asked Alan, "that you have a certain mixture that has—er—quite extraordinary effects?"

"My dear sir," replied the old man, "my stock in trade is not very large—but it is varied. Nothing I sell has effects which could be described as usual."

"Well the fact is—" began Alan.

"Here for example," interrupted the old man, reaching for a bottle from the shelf. "Here is a liquid as colorless as water, impossible to taste in coffee, milk, or any other beverage. It is also impossible to ever discover or detect."

"Do you mean it is a poison?" cried Alan, horrified.

"Call it a glove cleaner if you like," said the old man

150

coolly. "Maybe it will clean gloves. I have never tried. One might call it a life cleaner. Lives need cleaning sometimes."

"I want nothing of that sort," said Alan.

"Probably it is just as well," said the old man. "Do you know the price of this? For one teaspoonful, which is sufficient, I ask five thousand dollars. Never less. Not a penny less."

"I hope all your mixtures are not as expensive," said Alan, looking worried.

"Oh dear, no," said the old man. "It would be no good charging that sort of price for a love potion, for example. Young people who need a love potion very seldom have five thousand dollars. Otherwise they would not need a love potion."

"I am glad to hear that," said Alan.

"I look at it like this," said the old man. "Please a customer with one article, and he will come back when he needs another. Even if it is more costly. He will save up for it, if necessary."

"So," said Alan, "you really do sell love potions."

"If I did not sell love potions," said the old man, reaching for another bottle, "I should not have mentioned the other matter to you."

"And these love potions," said Alan. "They are not just—just—er—"

"Oh, no," said the old man. "Their effects are permanent. They last forever."

"Dear me!" said Alan. "How very interesting!"

"Give one tiny bit of this to the young lady, and she will change altogether. She will want nothing but quiet and you."

"I can hardly believe it," said Alan. "She is so fond of parties."

"She will not like them anymore," said the old man. "She will be afraid of the pretty girls you may meet."

"She will actually be jealous," cried Alan, delighted. "Of me?"

"Yes. She will want to be everything to you."

"She is, already. Only she doesn't care about it."

"She will, when she has taken this. She will care intensely. You will be her only interest in life."

"Wonderful!" cried Alan.

"She will want to know all you do," said the old man. "All that has happened to you during the day. Every word of it.

She will want to know what you are thinking about, why you smile suddenly, why you are looking sad."

"That is love!" cried Alan.

"Yes," said the old man. "How carefully she will look after you! She will never allow you to be tired, to sit in a draft, to eat too little. If you are an hour late, she will be terrified. She will think you are killed."

"It is hard to imagine Diana like that!" cried Alan, filled with joy.

"You will not have to use your imagination," said the old man. "No, you need not worry. She will want to be with you always. She will never, never leave you. Oh, no."

"And how much," said Alan, "is this wonderful mixture?"

"It is not as expensive," said the old man, "as the glove cleaner, or life cleaner, as I sometimes call it. No. That is five thousand dollars, never a penny less. One has to be older than you are to get that sort of thing. One has to save up for it."

"But the love potion?" asked Alan.

"Oh, that," said the old man. He opened the drawer in the kitchen table and took out a tiny bottle. "That is just a dollar."

"I can't tell you how grateful I am," said Alan, watching the old man fill the bottle.

> Now it's time for YOU to be The Reader as Detective.
>
> What do you think the old man will say to Alan? Clues in the story should help you answer correctly. Read on to see if you are right.

"I like to oblige," said the old man. "Then customers come back, later in life, when they are better off, and want more expensive things. Here you are. You will find it very effective."

"Thank you again," said Alan. "Good-bye."

"Be seeing you," said the old man.

Be The Reader as Detective again.

Why did the old man charge so little for the love potion? What does he think is going to happen?

I. The Reader as Detective

Read each of the following questions. Then write the letter of the correct answer to each question. Remember, the symbol next to each question identifies the *kind* of reading skill that particular question helps you to develop.

1. How much did the love potion cost?

   a. one dollar
   b. five dollars
   c. five thousand dollars

2. Which of the following is true of the "glove cleaner"?

   a. It had a bitter taste.
   b. It was colorless.
   c. It was easy to discover, or detect.

3. It is correct to infer that

   a. Diana was very much in love with Alan.
   b. Alan didn't love Diana.
   c. Alan was in love with Diana, but she didn't love him.

4. The old man said that his "stock in trade" was not very large. As used in this sentence, the word *stock* means

   a. shares in a company.
   b. items for sale.
   c. wooden frame.

5. Which happened last?

   a. Alan gave the old man a card.
   b. The old man took a tiny bottle from a drawer.
   c. Alan thanked the old man.

6. The old man's room

   a. was very fancy.

   b. was filled with furniture.

   c. contained a table and two chairs.

7. "She will never allow you to be tired, to sit in a draft, to eat too little." In this sentence, the word *draft* means

   a. current of air.

   b. rough copy.

   c. bank check.

8. According to Alan, Diana liked

   a. reading.

   b. parties.

   c. going to museums.

9. Which of the following is a fact?

   a. Alan and Diana will live happily ever after.

   b. Diana often asked Alan why he was looking sad.

   c. The story takes place near Pell Street.

10. "The Chaser" makes the point that

   a. everyone should try to buy a love potion.

   b. love always lasts forever.

   c. a satisfied customer always comes back.

II. On the Trail

PREDICTING EVENTS

Sometimes, clues in a story suggest events which will happen in the future. By using these clues, the reader as detective can predict the events.

How good are you at seeing in advance, or *predicting events*? The following questions will help you practice this skill.

11. Based on what happens in the story, we can predict that

   a. Diana will never see Alan again.

   b. Diana will fall in love with Alan.

   c. the old man will raise the price of the love potion.

12. The author suggests that Alan

    a. will become rich and famous.
    b. will eventually grow tired of Diana.
    c. will love Diana forever.

13. Which sentence best tells how Diana will feel about Alan?

    a. She will not like him very much.
    b. She will soon lose interest in him.
    c. She will make him the center of her life.

14. It is fair to predict that Alan will

    a. change jobs.
    b. never see the old man again.
    c. return to buy the "glove cleaner."

15. Clues in the story suggest that one day Alan will

    a. save Diana's life.
    b. become a murderer.
    c. tell the police about the old man.

III. Finding Word Meanings

Listed below are five vocabulary words which appear in "The Chaser" and five *new* vocabulary words for you to learn. Study the words and their definitions. Then complete the following paragraphs by using each vocabulary word only *once*.

		page
extraordinary	out of the usual	150
varied	unlike; different	150
liquid	something that flows easily and changes shape, like water	150
sufficient	enough; as much as is needed	152
permanent	lasting forever	152
seek	try to find; search for	
centuries	hundreds of years	
suggestion	idea; hint	
absorbed	greatly interested in; taken up fully with	
properly	correctly	

Throughout history, people have been __16__ with the idea of staying young. This was a strong interest of the Spanish explorer, Ponce de Léon. More than four __17__ ago, he set sail in search of the Fountain of Youth. According to stories, just one sip of the __18__ from this fountain was __19__ to keep the drinker forever young.

Ponce de Léon never found this amazing, __20__ fountain, of course. But that has not stopped people from continuing to __21__ unusual and __22__ ways of remaining young. Probably, there is no magic secret for bringing about __23__ and never-ending youth. But here is a helpful __24__ . If you stay fit, exercise regularly, and eat __25__ and well, you are likely to feel youthful much longer.

IV. Reviewing the Case

Now it's time to review the case. Pretend that a year has passed, and that Alan has returned to see the old man. Write what you think Alan would say to him. Be sure to put quotation marks around Alan's words.

Afterwards, you may have an opportunity to share your writing with the class, and to select the most interesting compositions.

> "And so, which will it be? Murderer or hero? My fate hangs on the edge of this razor blade."

Lather and Nothing Else

by Hernando Tellez

He came in without a word. I was stropping* my best razor. And when I recognized him, I started to shake. But he did not notice. To cover my nervousness, I went on honing the razor. I tried the edge with the tip of my thumb and took another look at it against the light.

Meanwhile, he was taking off his cartridge-studded belt with the pistol holster suspended from it. He put it on a hook in the wardrobe and hung his cap above it. Then he turned full around toward me and, loosening his tie, remarked: "It's hot as the devil. I want a shave." With that he took his seat.

I estimated he had a four-days' growth of beard. The four days he had been gone on the last foray† after our men. His face looked burnt, tanned by the sun.

I started to work carefully on the shaving soap. I scraped some slices from the cake, dropped them into the mug, then added a little lukewarm water and stirred with the brush. The lather soon began to rise.

"The fellows in the troop must have just about as much beard as I." I went on stirring up lather.

"But we did very well, you know. We caught the leaders.

---

*stropping: sharpening by sliding back and forth on a strap.
†foray: a sudden attack or raid.

158

Some of them we brought back dead; others are still alive. But they'll all be dead soon."

"How many did you take?" I asked.

"Fourteen. We had to go pretty far in to find them. But now they're paying for it. And not one will escape; not a single one."

He leaned back in the chair when he saw the brush in my hand, full of lather. I had not yet put the sheet on him. I was certainly flustered. Taking a sheet from the drawer, I tied it around my customer's neck.

He went on talking. He evidently took it for granted I was on the side of the existing regime.*

"The people must have gotten a scare with what happened the other day," he said.

"Yes," I replied, as I finished tying the knot against his nape, which smelt of sweat.

"Good show, wasn't it?"

"Very good," I answered, turning my attention now to the brush. The man closed his eyes wearily and awaited the cool caress of the lather.

I had never had him so close before. The day he ordered the people to file through the schoolyard to look upon the four rebels hanging there, my path had crossed his briefly. But the sight of those mutilated bodies kept me from paying attention to the face of the man who had been directing it all and whom I now had in my hands.

It was not a disagreeable face, certainly. And the beard, which aged him a bit, was not unbecoming. His name was Torres. Captain Torres.

I started to lay on the first coat of lather. He kept his eyes closed.

"I would love to catch a nap," he said, "but there's a lot to be done this evening."

I lifted the brush and asked, with pretended indifference: "A firing party?"

"Something of the sort," he replied, "but slower."

"All of them?"

"No, just a few."

I went on lathering his face. My hands began to tremble

---

*regime: the government in power.

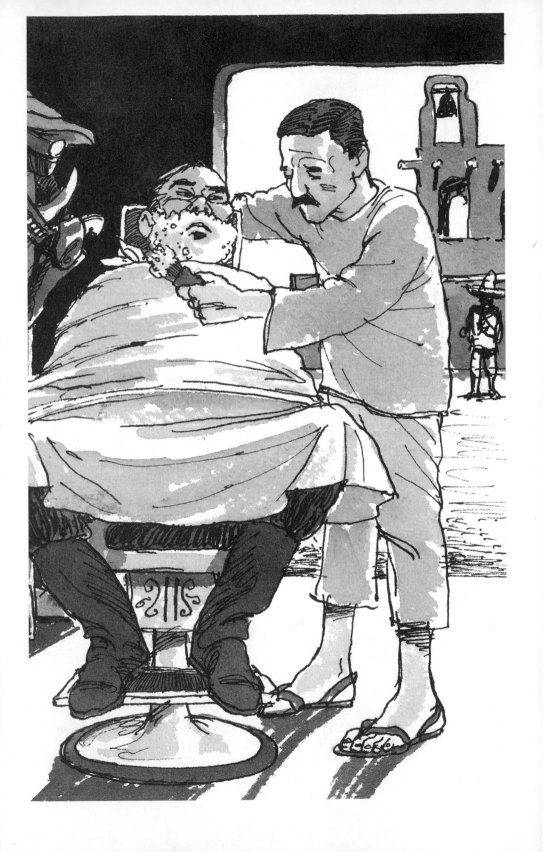

again. The man could not be aware of this, which was lucky for me. But I wished he had not come in. Probably many of our men had seen him enter the shop. And with the enemy in my house I felt a certain responsibility.

I would have to shave his beard just like any other, carefully, neatly, just as though he were a good customer, taking heed that not a single pore should emit a drop of blood. Seeing to it that the blade did not slip in the small whorls. Taking care that the skin was left clean, soft, shining, so that when I passed the back of my hand over it, not a single hair should be felt. Yes. I was secretly a revolutionary,* but at the same time I was a conscientious barber, proud of the way I did my job. And that four-day beard presented a challenge.

I took up the razor, opened the handle wide, releasing the blade, and started to work, downward from one sideburn. The blade responded to perfection. The hair was tough and hard; not very long, but thick. Little by little the skin began to show through. The razor gave out its usual sound as it gathered up layers of soap mixed with bits of hair. I paused to wipe it clean, and taking up the strop once more went about improving its edge, for I am a painstaking barber.

The man, who had kept his eyes closed, now opened them, put a hand out from under the sheet, felt of the part of his face that was emerging from the lather, and said to me: "Come at six o'clock this evening to the school."

"Will it be like the other day?" I asked, stiff with horror.

"It may be even better," he replied.

"What are you planning to do?"

"I'm not sure yet. But we'll have a good time."

Once more he leaned back and shut his eyes. I came closer, the razor on high.

"Are you going to punish all of them?" I timidly ventured.

"Yes, all of them."

The lather was drying on his face. I must hurry. Through the mirror, I took a look at the street. It appeared about as usual: there was the grocery shop with two or three customers. Then I glanced at the clock: two-thirty.

The razor kept descending. Now from the other sideburn

---

*revolutionary: one who tries to overthrow the government in power.

downward. It was a blue beard, a thick one. He should let it grow like some poets, or some priests. It would suit him well. Many people would not recognize him. And that would be a good thing for him, I thought, as I went gently over all the throat line. At this point you really had to handle your blade skillfully, because the hair, while scantier, tended to fall into small whorls. It was a curly beard. The pores might open, minutely, in this area and let out a tiny drop of blood. A good barber like myself stakes his reputation on not permitting that to happen to any of his customers.

And this was indeed a special customer. How many of ours had he sent to their death? How many had he mutilated? It was best not to think about it. Torres did not know I was his enemy. Neither he nor the others knew it. It was a secret shared by very few, just because that made it possible for me to inform the revolutionaries about Torres' activities in the town and what he planned to do every time he went on one of his raids to hunt down rebels. So it was going to be very difficult to explain how it was that I had him in my hands and then let him go in peace, alive, clean-shaven.

His beard had now almost entirely disappeared. He looked younger, several years younger than when he had come in. I suppose that always happens to men who enter and leave barber shops. Under the strokes of my razor Torres was rejuvenated;* yes, because I am a good barber, the best in this town, and I say this in all modesty.

A little more lather here under the chin, on the Adam's apple, right near the great vein. How hot it is! Torres must be sweating just as I am. But he is not afraid. He is a tranquil man, who is not even giving thought to what he will do to his prisoners this evening. I, on the other hand, polishing his skin with this razor but avoiding the drawing of blood, careful with every stroke—I cannot keep my thoughts in order.

Confound the hour he entered my shop! I am a revolutionary but not a murderer. And it would be so easy to kill him. He deserves it. Or does he? No. No one deserves the sacrifice others make in becoming assassins. What is to be gained by it? Nothing. Others and still others keep coming, and the first kill the second, and then these kill the next, and so on until

---

*rejuvenated: made to appear young and fresh again.

everything becomes a sea of blood. I could cut his throat, so, swish, swish! He would not even have time to moan, and with his eyes shut he would not even see the shine of the razor or the gleam in my eye.

I'm sure that with a good strong blow, a deep cut, he would feel no pain. He would not suffer at all. And what would I do then with the body? Where would I hide it? I would have to flee, leave all this behind, take shelter far away, very far away. But they would follow until they caught up with me. "The murderer of Captain Torres. He slit his throat while he was shaving him. What a cowardly thing to do!"

And others would say: "The avenger* of our people. A name to remember"—my name here. "He was the town barber. No one knew he was fighting for our cause."

And so, which will it be? Murderer or hero? My fate hangs on the edge of this razor blade. I can turn my wrist slightly, put a bit more pressure on the blade, let it sink in. The skin will yield like silk. like rubber, like the strop. There is nothing more tender than a man's skin, and the blood is always there, ready to burst forth. A razor like this cannot fail. It is the best one I have.

But I don't want to be a murderer. No, sir. You came in to be shaved. And I do my work honorably. I don't want to stain my hands with blood. Just with lather, and nothing else. You are an executioner; I am only a barber. Each one to his job. That's it. Each one to his job.

The chin was now clean, polished, soft. The man got up and looked at himself in the glass. He ran his hand over the skin and felt its freshness, its newness.

"Thanks," he said. He walked to the wardrobe for his belt, his pistol, and his cap. I must have been very pale, and I felt my shirt soaked with sweat. Torres finished adjusting his belt buckle, straightened his gun in its holster, and, smoothing his hair mechanically, put on his cap. From his trousers pocket he took some coins to pay for the shave. And he started toward the door. On the threshold he stopped for a moment, and turning toward me he said:

---

*avenger: one who punishes a wrongdoer.

Now it's time for YOU to be the Reader as Detective.

What do you think Captain Torres said to the barber? Read on to see if you are right.

"They told me you would kill me. I came to find out if it was true. But it's not easy to kill. I know what I'm talking about."

I. The Reader as Detective

Read each of the following questions. Then write the letter of the correct answer to each question. Remember, the symbol next to each question identifies the *kind* of reading skill that particular question helps you to develop.

 1. How many prisoners did Captain Torres take?

   a. four   *b.* fourteen   *c.* forty

 2. When does the story take place?

   a. at noon   *c.* at five o'clock
   b. around two-thirty

 3. We may infer that Captain Torres knew that the barber

   a. was his enemy.
   b. would refuse to shave him.
   c. would give him a poor shave.

 4. When Captain Torres came in, the barber was stropping his best razor. The word *stropping* means

   a. selling.   *b.* folding.   *c.* sharpening.

 5. Captain Torres had

   a. a long, flowing beard.
   b. a thick, blue beard.
   c. a white mustache.

6. What did Captain Torres do first?

a. He took off his cartridge belt and his cap.

b. He took some coins from his pocket to pay for the shave.

c. He told the barber to come to the school at six o'clock.

7. The barber told the revolutionaries

a. where Captain Torres lived.

b. where the leaders were hiding.

c. about Captain Torres's raids.

8. The barber stated, "I don't want to stain my hands with blood." The word *stain* means

a. wash.

b. make beautiful.

c. spot or disgrace.

9. In which of the following quotations does the storyteller express an opinion?

a. "I am a good barber, the best in town."

b. "His beard had now almost entirely disappeared."

c. "My hands began to tremble again."

10. Which of the following would make the best title for the story?

a. A Four-Day Beard

b. How to Shave a Customer

c. The Captain and the Barber

II. On the Trail

DISCERNING CHARACTER

There are only two characters in "Lather and Nothing Else." Understanding the *characterization* of each will help you better enjoy and appreciate the story.

Answer the following questions. Each one deals with characterization.

11. Which group of words best describes the barber?

　　a. thoughtful, nervous
　　b. fearless, calm
　　c. careless, selfish

12. How did the barber feel about the government in power?

　　a. He took no interest in the government.
　　b. He was opposed to, or against, the government.
　　c. He was on the side of the government.

13. Based on his actions, it is correct to state that Captain Torres was

　　a. a coward.
　　b. a brave man.
　　c. planning to kill the barber.

14. The barber was

　　a. proud of his work.
　　b. ashamed of his work.
　　c. not too careful with the razor.

15. Which of the following statements is true?

　　a. The barber discovered that it was easy for him to become a murderer.
　　b. Captain Torres believed that it is easy to take the life of another man.
　　c. The barber learned what Captain Torres knew: it is not easy to kill.

III. Finding Word Meanings

　　The ten words listed below appear in "Lather and Nothing Else." Study the words and their definitions. Then complete the following paragraphs by using each vocabulary word only *once*.

		page
razor	a tool used for shaving	158
foray	an attack or a raid	158
regime	system of government	159
disagreeable	not to one's liking; unpleasant	159

		page
revolutionary	one who wants to overthrow the government in power	161
perfection	of the very best; of the highest quality; completely without fault	161
rebels	people who fight instead of obeying	162
tranquil	calm	162
pressure	force or weight	163
executioner	a person hired to put criminals or lawbreakers to death; a murderer	163

"Lather and Nothing Else" is about a barber who is secretly a __16__ ; that is, he is an enemy of the government in power. One afternoon, Captain Torres visits the barber shop. The captain is a member of the local government, or __17__ . He has just returned from a __18__ hunting down a group of __19__ .

The captain appears very calm and __20__ as the barber shaves him. The barber, on the other hand, trembles with nervousness. He knows that by putting a little __21__ on the blade of his __22__ , he can easily kill his enemy.

However, the thought of killing the captain soon becomes unpleasant and __23__ . The barber finally gives the captain an excellent shave, one which is __24__ itself. He has decided that he is a barber—not a killer or __25__ .

IV. Reviewing the Case

Now it's time to review the case. In two or three sentences for each, explain why you agree *or* disagree with the statements below. Begin the first sentence of each answer with the words, *"I agree" or "I disagree."*

A. The barber should have killed Captain Torres.
B. Captain Torres was a fool to let the barber shave him.
C. Captain Torres didn't know that the barber was a revolutionary.

Afterwards, you may have an opportunity to compare your answers with those of your classmates. It will be interesting to discover how many agree or disagree with you, and which points of view prove most popular.

GLOSSARY

A

absorbed   greatly interested in; taken up fully with
abundant   many; more than enough
accurate   without errors; correct
achievement   something carried out successfully
active   lively; showing much attention
additional   extra; added; more
adjusts   gets used to
advice   opinion about what to do
alert   wide-awake; very watchful
amusement   pleasure
anticipated   expected
apologized   offered an excuse; said one is sorry
appreciated   thought highly of; valued
argument   a talk, or discussion, by people who do not agree with
   each other
arresting   very striking; holding one's attention
assassins   murderers
assistance   help
astounded   greatly surprised
attaché   a person on the staff of a minister or similar official
attempt   make an effort; try

B

beloved   dearly loved
bleachers   benches or stands for the fans at sporting events
bragging   praising or boasting about oneself
brilliant   very bright

C

career   life's work; way of living
cartridge   a case for holding bullets or ammunition
caution   warning
centuries   hundred of years
chill   make cold; sudden coldness
coincidence   the chance happening of two things in such a way as
   to be striking or unusual
companion   one who shares in what another is doing
compartments   separate sections of spaces

168

compete   try to win something wanted by others
complaint   a finding of fault; finding fault
comprehend   understand
conceal   hide; keep secret
conclusions   opinions reached through reasoning
confidence   strong belief in oneself
confound   cause ruin or shame; curse
congratulate   to show pleasure to someone who has been success-
    ful or lucky
connection   joining together
conscientious   very careful; acting in a manner one knows is right
consider   think about; keep in mind
considerable   not a little; much
construct   put together; build
control   hold back; have power over
conversation   friendly talk
conveyed   carried; made known
created   brought into being; made
crisis   a very difficult or important event or time
critic   a person who judges or gives opinions

D

daze   state of being unable to think clearly
demonstrated   showed
described   told or pictured in words
despair   loss of hope
detail   small part
detected   discovered
devoted   faithful; loyal
diploma   a document, or official paper, given to a person upon
    graduation
disagreeable   not to one's liking; unpleasant
discouraging   causing to lose hope
discussion   a talk between two or more people
distinction   honor
disturbing   upsetting

E

effectively   with skill or ability
embarrassed   made uneasy and ashamed
emerge   come out; come into view
enchanted   magic
energy   strength or power

entirely   completely
exaggerating   going beyond the truth
exceedingly   very; very greatly
executioner   a person hired to put criminals or lawbreakers to death; a murderer
extraordinary   out of the usual

F

fantasy   a story that takes place in one's mind
fascinating   of very great interest
fatal   causing death or ruin
fictional   made up
flustered   mixed up
foray   an attack or a raid
former   the first of two
furnished   supplied

G

gesture   any movement or action that shows feeling
gilt   golden in color
granted   given; awarded
groove   a channel or rut

H

hideous   horrible; frightful
honing   sharpening
hostess   a woman who receives another person or other persons as her guest(s)
hysterical   highly excited; out of self-control

I

immensely   very greatly
impressed   had a strong effect on; moved
indicate   show; say
indifference   not caring; lack of interest
indirectly   not directly connected
influence   having an effect on others
initial   earliest; first
innocent   doing no harm; simple
inscription   written words
inspection   the act of looking at closely
intelligence   ability to learn and know

intent   strong purpose; strongly fixed on something
introduction   beginning or starting point; making known
investigation   a careful search
invisible   not able to be seen
involved   interested in

J

jousting   combat between armed knights on horseback

K

keen   sharp

L

liable   likely to
liquid   something that flows easily and changes shape, like water
lobby   entrance hall
lounging   passing time lazily
luxurious   comfortable and pleasant

M

member   a person belonging to a group
mocking   making fun of
mutilated   torn apart; broken

N

nasty   mean or cruel
naturalist   a person who studies animals and plants
needless   not needed; not necessary
numerous   many

O

observe   see and note; study
obtaining   getting
obvious   easily seen or understood
occurs   happens
ordinary   common; not special

P

peculiar   strange
pension   regular payment of money for long service to someone
    who has reached a certain age

perfection   of the very best; of the highest quality; completely without fault

periscope   an instrument on a submarine for viewing the surface of the water.

permanent   lasting forever

pleasure   enjoyment; delight

pollution   the dirtying of conditions that affect the growth of life

popular   liked by most people

positive   certain; sure

preferred   liked better; chose

pressure   force of weight

prevent   stop; keep from happening

probable   likely to happen; likely to be true

produced   brought forth

properly   correctly

provide   offer up; supply

purloined   stolen

R

razor   a tool used for shaving

reaction   an answer, by word or deed, to some action

rebels   people who fight instead of obeying

recent   done not long ago; not long past

recollection   memory

reflect   think carefully

regime   system of government

rejected   refused

reliable   worthy of trust; able to depend upon

remarkable   unusual

reputation   good name; fame

responsibility   a task or job that one is expected to do

retire   rest; give up a job because of age

revolutionary   one who wants to overthrow the government in power

ridiculous   deserving to be made fun of; laughable; silly

routine   usual; average

rupees   units of money used in India and certain other countries

S

satisfying   pleasing; enjoyable

scars   marks left by a wound

seek   try to find; search for

sequence a connected series
shame feeling of disgrace; pity
shudder shake with fear
similar alike; much the same
sluggish slow-moving
sneer look intended to make one feel low or worthless
soothingly calmly; quietly
sore angry; painful
spacious containing much space; large
speckled marked with small spots
spellbound too interested to move
splendid very fine; excellent
stammered spoke slowly and haltingly because of nervousness
stashed hid
static noises usually caused by electrical problems
steady changing little; firm
stroll to walk slowly and easily
stunts acts that draw attention
style quality
sufficient enough; as much as is needed
suggestion idea; hint
survey to look over
swirling moving with a twisting motion

T

threat sign or cause of harm
thrilled excited
tone manner of speaking or writing
tradition something, such as a custom, which has been handed
down from parents to children
tragedy a terrible happening; unusual sadness
tranquil calm
trio group of three
triumph success; victory
typical of a type; a good example

U

uncertainty showing doubt
undisguised not hidden; open
undisturbed not bothered; calm
undoubtedly without question
unnatural strange; shocking

V

vaguest   slightest; very unclear
varied   unlike; different
vast   very great
vehicle   any means of carrying, communicating, or making known
ventilation   something which lets in fresh air
veranda   a large porch
victim   a person injured or badly treated
vivid   lively; clear; distinct

W

whorls   circles